The Truth about Science

A Curriculum for Developing Young Scientists

By Kathryn Kelsey and Ashley Steel

National Science Teachers Association

Art and Design
Linda Olliver, Director
NSTA Web
Tim Weber, Webmaster
Periodicals Publishing
Shelley Carey, Director
Printing and Production
Catherine Lorrain-Hale, Director
Publications Operations
Erin Miller, Manager
*sci*LINKS
Tyson Brown, Manager

National Science Teachers Association
Gerald F. Wheeler, Executive Director
David Beacom, Publisher

NSTA Press, NSTA Journals, and the NSTA website deliver high-quality resources for science educators.

Shirley Watt Ireton, Director
Judy Cusick, Associate Editor
Carol Duval, Associate Editor
Linda Olliver, Cover Design
    and Illustration

Featuring *sci*LINKS®—a new way of connecting text and the Internet. Up-to-the-minute online content, classroom ideas, and other materials are just a click away. Go to page xxx to learn more about this new educational resource.

The Truth about Science: A Curriculum for Developing Young Scientists
NSTA Stock Number: PB164X
ISBN: 0-87355-189-2
Library of Congress Control Number: 2001097577
Printed in the USA by Banta Book Group–Harrisonburg
Printed on recycled paper

Table of Contents

SECTION I: Research Questions and Hypotheses

SECTION II: Experimental Design

SECTION III: Summarizing and Analyzing Results

SECTION IV: Presentation of Research Projects

About the Authors

Kathryn Kelsey has a B.A. in human biology, an M.A. in secondary science education, and a Ph.D. in wildlife ecology. Currently, she teaches high school science and acts as a middle school science resource teacher for the Seattle Public Schools. She is also co-director of the Science Inquiry and Research Council in Seattle. She worked as a research scientist in wildlife ecology before bringing her experience as a scientist back into the secondary school classroom in Seattle. Her first teaching experiences were in Bénin and New York City.

Ashley Steel has M.S. degrees in both river ecology and statistics and a Ph.D. in quantitative ecology. She is currently a quantitative ecologist with the Watershed Program at the Northwest Fisheries Science Center and co-director of the Science Inquiry and Research Council in Seattle. Her teaching experience includes working at academic summer programs, visiting schools as a guest scientist, and pilot teaching *The Truth about Science* in the Seattle Public Schools. Ashley was also a Luce Scholar in Thailand, where she initiated and taught a student river-monitoring program.

Preface

Welcome to *The Truth about Science: A Curriculum for Developing Young Scientists*. These lessons for middle schoolers combine hands-on activities with a student-designed research project to develop the thinking and research skills used by scientists. The approach integrates creative thinking, critical thinking, problem solving, reading, writing, and mathematics.

We developed the module in two pilot classrooms, tested it in four others, and trained more than 30 additional teachers to field test it. Feedback from all teachers using the curriculum has been incorporated into this edition. Countless young scientists have successfully completed the curriculum. We invite you to use it and provide your students with an opportunity to do real science research.

Comments and suggestions on the curriculum are available on *The Truth about Science* webpage at *www.nrcse.washington.edu/truth*. We intend to monitor this page and display communications from curriculum users as long as possible. Please feel free to contact us through the webpage with your feedback.

—Kathryn Kelsey and Ashley Steel

Acknowledgments

We would like to extend our thanks to all the people who have facilitated the development of this project. In particular, we thank Greg Coy and the board of the Discuren Foundation and Peter Guttorp and the board of the National Research Center for Statistics and the Environment for providing financial support; June Morita for serving as the principal investigator on our first grant and for providing inspiration and critical reviews; John Miner, Rick Lemberg, and Vivian Scheidt at AE (Alternative Elementary) #2; Cathy Hayes, Marty Christianson, and Patty Gale at Summit K–12; Kris Chorskie and Kylie Rehrig at Blaine School; Caroline Kiehle and the Middle School Science Systemic Reform Project; University of Washington graduate students Mike Johnson, Liz Ritzenthaler, Eriko Rossano, Chrissy Scannell, and Emily Silverman; Gerri Goedde for providing administrative support; Jay Milton for the design and layout of the pre-published curriculum; Leina Johansson for assistance with last-minute document management; and all the students and parents who have been instrumental in supporting and implementing this project.

At NSTA, Judy Cusick was the project editor for the book. Linda Olliver designed the book and its cover. Catherine Lorrain-Hale laid out the book and coordinated production and printing.

Introduction

Our primary goal in *The Truth about Science: A Curriculum for Developing Young Scientists* is to introduce students to the process of scientific research. Many people regard science as a body of knowledge that describes the natural world. How many also think of science as the process through which that knowledge was developed? Students who complete *The Truth about Science* will. With this curriculum, they make qualitative and quantitative observations and think creatively about the relationships of and influences on what they observe. They develop a testable research question and hypotheses, identify pertinent background information, and design an experiment to answer their specific research question. Through the process of science research, they practice techniques to randomize sampling, to control for unwanted effects, and to standardize methods so they can be replicated. After collecting data, student investigators summarize, analyze, and interpret the data; place results in the context of the larger body of science knowledge; review research reports written by peers; and present research results to a live audience. These are skills students will draw on in future science classes as well as in work settings.

The Truth about Science attempts to fill several gaps in science education. As teachers and as students, we have found that students rarely get an opportunity to be scientists, that is, to ask and answer their own scientific questions. In English classes, most students have an opportunity to be authors of fiction and nonfiction works. History teachers encourage students to synthesize points of view and write essays on historical issues just as historians do. It is true that in hands-on science classes and science labs students learn lab techniques and demonstrate how something works. Rarely, however, do they get a chance to think creatively and to apply the techniques they have learned to a research project or an experiment of their own design. We have written this curriculum to provide middle school students with an opportunity to do their own science research, just as more senior scientists do.

The curriculum also attempts to subvert a common misconception of students—that they will never use the skills learned in math classes. Mathematics is a critical tool used by scientists all the time! The curriculum approaches data analysis from a statistical perspective. Students learn to summarize and represent their data using averages, tables, and graphs. They learn how variability in data influences interpretations and how to assess and display variance. These methods push students to think analytically and critically about their data and their Long-Term Research Projects (LTRPs).

We reward students for all of their creativity, critical thinking, and hard work by hosting a final celebration where they display posters and give short oral presentations on their research projects. Families, teachers, and administrators are all invited to celebrate and congratulate the students on their accomplishments. Scientists have a responsibility to report their results to the larger scientific community and the general public. This new generation of scientists will have experienced this critical step of the scientific process by the time they have completed middle school.

Organization

The curriculum is designed to be taught from beginning to end (Day 1 to Day 40). For the teacher with limited time, however, we outline three "Fast-Track" options on pages ix–xi. Overall, the curriculum presents scientific inquiry skills in a sequentially logical manner and creates opportunities for students to practice and apply the skills in a research project of their own. The centerpiece of the curriculum is the Long-Term Research Project (LTRP), in which student groups formulate a testable research question and hypotheses, design their experimental methods, collect and analyze data, and present their research results and conclusions in a written and oral format.

The Long-Term Research Project directs students to develop field ecology research projects at a local park or in the school yard. Because the purpose of the curriculum is to develop science process skills, however, the teacher can direct students to develop lab- or field-based Long-Term Research Projects within any science discipline (see pages 38–39 for ideas on other science avenues to pursue). Teachers who feel pressure to cover a specific subject can focus the Long-Term Research Projects more narrowly and include more content material to support the projects. For example, students doing ecology-based projects in the school yard can spend time learning about leaf structure, photosynthesis, tree physiology, and the water cycle before finalizing their research questions and methods.

The curriculum is divided into four sections; each section contains several pages of background information and approximately 10 lessons.

Section I: Research Questions and Hypotheses. Days 1–10.

The first section guides students to ask testable questions, and formulate hypotheses and null hypotheses. Students also become familiar with the parts of a science research report. This structure reinforces the concepts of quantitative observations and comparative research. It also sets the stage for doing statistical testing. At the end of the first section, students are ready to ask a research question and formulate hypotheses for their Long-Term Research Projects. Students finish the section by drafting the introduction paragraphs for their LTRP poster presentations.

Section II: Experimental Design. Days 11–20.

The second section emphasizes concepts of experimental design. Students conduct two experiments and observe how changes in the procedures influence the results. They learn from experience the concepts of treatment and control, replication, randomization, and controlling for factors that might influence results. These concepts help students to design objective experiments and avoid investigator bias. With this background, they return to their small groups and design experiments to answer their earlier research questions. At this point, students draft the methods paragraph for their LTRP poster presentations. The final two lessons provide time for the students to collect data for their research projects. Data collection could involve a field trip to the school yard or to a park.

Section III: Summarizing and Analyzing Results. Days 21–32.

This third section emphasizes quantitative skills used to understand data sets. The lessons include data analysis and data interpretation. Students learn to summarize data using averages, to display data using histograms, to evaluate the impact of data variability on conclusions, and to conduct and interpret statistical tests. The quantitative skills are taught through hands-on activities and are then applied to the students' own data sets. At the conclusion of this section, students draft their results paragraph, describing their graphs and data analysis, and their discussion paragraph, interpreting and concluding the projects. We have included plenty of background information and references for teachers who have not had much experience with statistics or quantitative analyses of data sets.

Section IV: Presentation of Research Projects. Days 33–40

Students put their posters together and prepare their oral presentations. It is wonderful to watch the groups work together in these final days. Motivation is high, creativity is soaring, and all the hard work of the previous weeks is paying off. Students are given an opportunity to review and critique each other's work and then to incorporate the suggestions into their final products. Students practice their presentations alone and in front of their own class before going on stage in front of their parents. The final celebration is just that, a celebration. This night, the students truly shine as they reveal the truth about science as they have experienced it.

Fast-Track Options

Teachers who do not have the 8 to 10 weeks required to complete the entire curriculum can still provide a worthy experience for their students. Here we present three Fast-Track options.

FAST-TRACK OPTION #1

This shortest version of the curriculum requires 10 days to teach science research concepts and to guide students to do a mini Long-Term Research Project (LTRP). In this modification of the curriculum, the students are exposed to the core processes of scientific research.

> Ooze Observations (Day 1)
> Science Boxes (Day 4)
> LTRP: Research Questions and Hypotheses (Day 8)
> The Toughest Towel (Days 11, 12) OR Wigglin' Worms (Days 13, 14)
> LTRP: Methods and Materials (Day 16)
> LTRP: Data Collection (Day 19)
> LTRP: Graphing Results (Days 22, 23)
> Writing Discussion Paragraphs (Day 31)

FAST-TRACK OPTION #2

The second Fast-Track option takes 15 days, and involves completing 12 lessons that build science research and inquiry skills. The Long-Term Research Project lessons are omitted. A teacher who needs to prepare students to do research projects for a local science fair might want to consider this option. The students learn the necessary concepts from these lessons and can then apply them to their science fair projects. The development of the science fair project may occur after completing the appropriate lessons in class.

Ooze Observations (Day 1)
Imagining and Planning Ooze Experiments (Day 2)
Ooze Experiments (Day 3)
Science Boxes (Days 4, 5)
    (Students can now write a testable research question for their science fair projects.)
The Toughest Towel (Days 11, 12)
Wigglin' Worms (Days 13, 14)
The Wheel of Inquiry Game! (Day 15)
    (Students can now design their experiments, write the methods, and collect data for their science fair projects.)
Aqueous Averages (Day 22)
Graphing Data (Day 23)
Faux Fish Figuring, Stat Savvy, and T-Test Practice (Days 25, 26, 27)
    (Students can now summarize and analyze data. They may need some guidelines for writing up their projects and preparing posters.)

FAST-TRACK OPTION #3

The third Fast-Track option takes 20 days, using 15 lessons, and supplements Fast-Track Option #1 with lessons that put the Long-Term Research Project research in context, review science process skills, provide additional insight into data interpretation, and guide students in preparing a research report.

Ooze Observations (Day 1)
Science Boxes (Day 4)
LTRP: Research Questions and Hypotheses (Day 8)
LTRP: Library Research I (Day 9)
LTRP: Introduction Paragraph (Day 10)
The Toughest Towel (Days 11, 12) OR Wigglin' Worms (Days 13, 14)
The Wheel of Inquiry Game! (Day 15)
LTRP: Methods and Materials (Day 16)
LTRP: Data Collection (Day 19)
LTRP: Graphing Results (Days 22, 23)
Writing Discussion Paragraphs (Day 31)
Faux Fish Figuring (Day 25)
LTRP: Results Paragraph (Day 28)
LTRP: Library Research II (Day 30)

LTRP: Poster Preparation (Days 34, 35, 36) or
      Oral Presentations (Days 37, 38, 39)
Celebration Night (or day)

Several other possible modifications are worth mentioning. The structure of the field trips (Days 19, 20) is flexible. We have written these lessons as two all-day field trips, but several afternoon trips to the school yard, one all-day trip and a follow-up half-day trip, or other combinations are also possible.

It should also be noted that the lessons on statistical analysis (Days 27, 28) may require extra time, particularly if students are not familiar with square roots or decimals. These lessons can be slowed down to emphasize the mathematical basics or they can be omitted if they seem overwhelming the first time through the curriculum. If you decide to omit these lessons, we recommend that the extra time be spent on Graphing Data (Days 23, 24), Faux Fish Figuring (Day 25), and Stat Savvy (Day 26).

Finally, it is difficult to have all groups ready for Peer Reviews (Day 33) at the same time. You may need to add a couple of catch-up days for groups who are behind in their writing before doing the Peer Review lesson.

Assessment of Student Learning

The Truth about Science includes both formative and summative assessment strategies. We place greater emphasis on formative assessments as these appear to be more important in raising student achievement than summative assessments (Black and Wiliam 1998). Formative assessments provide useful information to the teacher on student understanding and performance at a time when the teacher can intervene to bring a student or group of students back on track. The teacher also has time to rethink classroom management strategies and student group arrangements. The summative assessments in this curriculum motivate students to work hard. Although summative assessments occur only in the last eight lessons, they provide information to the teacher on overall mastery and effort.

FORMATIVE ASSESSMENTS

Formative assessments occur at the end of the first three sections of the curriculum. The lessons in each section focus on the development and implementation of a specific aspect of the research project. Project development culminates with the writing of each of the following paragraphs: Introduction (Day 10), Methods (Day 16), Results (Day 29), and Discussion (Days 31, 32). The paragraphs reflect each group's understanding of the research process and of its research project at that time. These are authentic assessments as every scientist must write up each of these sections when reporting research results.

Each of these lessons includes a scoring rubric to help teachers evaluate student work. The graded paragraph may reflect a group's best effort, reducing the number of paragraphs the teacher must read, or an individual's best effort. When students combine the four paragraphs, they create a complete research report or paper (minus the bibliography).

Another useful formative assessment occurs on Day 15, The Wheel of Inquiry Game! In playing this game, students review the concepts of science research that they have learned up to this point, and their responses to the game questions show the teacher which concepts continue to pose difficulties. We provide enough questions so that teachers can play the game several times with one class.

The Wigglin' Worms lesson (Days 13, 14) provides an opportunity for a performance-based formative assessment that checks students' ability to set up a controlled experiment. After completing The Toughest Towel lesson on the previous two days, students can apply the experimental protocols they learned with paper towels to worms. One teacher reported that she gave pairs of students 20 minutes to set up their worm experiments. This abbreviated time meant that those who clearly understood the concepts of experimental design would be able to set up the experiment correctly and those who did not would not have time to figure it out. The students not able to complete the task received more individual help to reinforce the concepts of experimental design. The teacher was ecstatic when 26 of 28 students successfully set up the experiment!

A final opportunity to use formative assessment occurs during the Peer Reviews lesson (Day 33). This assessment mirrors the responsibility real scientists have in reviewing reports written by colleagues before reports are accepted for publication. Critically reviewing the work of others in a constructive manner is an excellent learning tool. It requires students to apply the skills and concepts learned from doing their own research to an unfamiliar project. Students must evaluate the content in the report without having firsthand experience in planning, collecting, or analyzing the data. The reviews also help students think more critically about their own work. Suggestions for scoring this lesson as a formative assessment are given in the lesson.

Finally, each lesson includes at least six discussion questions, which can be used at the beginning or end of the class period. By systematically asking different students to respond to the questions, the teacher can obtain feedback as to student understanding.

SUMMATIVE ASSESSMENTS

Teachers can, of course, prepare traditional written quizzes and tests or assign homework based on the discussion questions at the end of each lesson. The ultimate summative assessment of student achievement, however, occurs at the conclusion of the project, when posters are put on public display and research groups give oral presentations detailing their research questions, methods, results, and conclusions. This is an obvious time for teacher and student evaluations of the work completed during the last two months. Teachers and students alike are accustomed to such end-of-unit graded products. Teachers and students can make the evaluations, or a panel of outside judges can review the posters or presentations (similar to a science fair). The teacher may also wish to evaluate science notebooks (which include all the Worksheets plus any other Long-Term Research Project notes). Presumably, the teacher has been checking the notebooks on a regular basis to ensure that all students are keeping up with the pace and completing all assignments. The teacher may provide students additional time to organize their notebooks before handing them in for a final grade.

SELF-ASSESSMENT

It is important for students to do self-evaluations of their contributions to the overall group project. Teachers may ask for self-evaluations at regular intervals or at the end of the curriculum. Self-evaluations give the teacher insight into group dynamics and the distribution of effort among individuals and allow students to reflect on their roles within the group. Providing more than one opportunity for this type of reflection may result in increased effort and investment.

ASSESSMENT SCENARIOS

To help teachers and students prepare for statewide science tests, we have included several scenario-based questions that assess understanding of scientific thinking, problem solving, and data interpretation (Appendix E). These questions are similar to The Wheel of Inquiry Game! (Day 15) questions, but are more structured. Teachers can ask a series of detailed questions about one scenario or combine several partial scenarios in a test. The scenarios emphasize the skills developed in each of the first three sections of the curriculum. The fourth section presents two summative assessments—project posters and oral presentations—and therefore no additional assessment questions are provided. Teachers can also choose to prepare multiple-choice or short-answer questions.

Planning Essentials

Materials

We have designed activities that use readily available, inexpensive materials. A complete materials list can be found on page xxv. Each student will also need a three-ring notebook (which we refer to throughout as the science notebook and into which students will put all completed Worksheets and other Long-Term Research Project notes) and a floppy computer disk. Each group will need a poster board for the group poster presentations during the last two weeks of the project.

Classroom Organization

The Long-Term Research Project requires more organization than many other classroom projects. Students should be aware of the project's scope from the beginning of the curriculum; their work is building toward a final celebration night complete with posters and oral presentations.

We have not included a lesson that introduces students to the goals of the curriculum. The teacher needs to find time to do this. One possibility is to incorporate an overall introduction into Ooze Experiments (Day 2), when students are introduced to the four parts of a scientific report.

The next step is to start thinking about how you will assign students to their Long-Term Research Project groups before carrying out the lesson LTRP: Research Questions and Hypotheses (Day 8). It works well to have students list their research interests by topic before LTRP: Field Techniques (Day 7). In interest groups (e.g., tree group, insect group, forest group, stream group), students can focus on field techniques that suit their potential projects. Then you can have students select their own groups within these interest groups, or you can have them list their first three choices for research projects and assign them to groups based on their choices and on which students you think will work best together.

Groups of three to four students work best. The workload is heavy for groups of only two students. On the other hand, groups of five or more tend to end up with some students doing all the work and others standing around. Large groups can also lead to boredom, infighting, and classroom chaos. At every opportunity, it will be helpful to remind students that if they have a group of four people, they need to have four people working.

As the Long-Term Research Projects progress, you will need a place in the classroom to keep track of group materials. Each group will have a computer disk, data, a poster, graphs, and paragraphs that don't belong to one student but rather to the whole group. If these get put in one student's notebook, it will be difficult for the rest of the group to work if that student is absent. As well, items tend to get lost if students forget which group member is keeping track of which item.

An important part of the Long-Term Research Project is keeping the paragraphs and data on the computer. The teacher should be comfortable saving files and using classroom software before the project begins. Making sure that each Long-Term Research Project group has a clearly labeled disk is very important. Files should be saved on the disk under descriptive names. Groups that save things as "Science1" and "Science2" end up spending a lot of time searching for files. Worse yet, groups that name everything "Science" end up with one file containing only the most recently saved work—everything else having been overwritten and consequently deleted. Names such as "Bug Intro" and "Bug Methods" are much more helpful. Computer etiquette and file management may need to be discussed as a class before students enter their introduction paragraphs into the computer (Day 10).

Selecting the Long-Term Research Project Site and Planning for Data Collection

If the class will be collecting data outdoors, the first step will be to select the field site. It needs to be chosen before the curriculum gets underway so that you can preview it for possible safety hazards and direct the students to develop appropriate research questions. The field site can be a local park or the school yard. The site selection should be based on convenience and ecological opportunities. The closer the site, the more time students have in the field for observing and collecting data. It is also easier to visit a nearby site before data collection begins to practice field techniques and to plan the Long-Term Research Projects. The more ecologically diverse the area, the more diverse and interesting the research projects. Long-Term Research Project sites with ponds, streams, forests, or beaches enable students to study ecological processes to which they may not be regularly exposed. Collecting aquatic insects or measuring tree density can be fun and memorable learning experiences.

Once the site is selected, start planning the field trips. Get parents involved; they can help with transportation (if necessary), assist student groups, and troubleshoot problems. One parent per student group eliminates lots of worries. You will need at least one data-collection field trip, but two or more will work better (Days 19, 20). If the field site is convenient to the school, you may also want to visit it to learn about the ecology of the site during Local Landscape (Day 6) and to learn about quantitative field techniques during LTRP: Field Techniques (Day 7).

Some teachers may wish to use the curriculum to do lab-based projects. In this case, the teacher must decide whether to limit topics and to what extent she or he will provide materials. If projects need to run for more than one day, does the classroom provide adequate space for all groups to store projects without taking them apart? Planning early will help reduce the number of last-minute details before students begin their data collection (Days 19, 20).

Lessons That Require Advance Planning

The first lesson that requires some advance preparation is Science Boxes (Days 4, 5). The teacher needs to prepare several boxes or large envelopes with objects and/or pictures from different ecosystems or for different science topics (see lesson plan for more details). You may want to collect materials for the science boxes when you first visit potential

Long-Term Research Project field sites or start researching your general topic. If you are planning a field trip, it will also be helpful to create a simple map of the site on the first visit. The map can be used during LTRP: Methods and Materials (Days 16, 17) to help students plan their data collection.

The second lesson that requires some extra planning is Local Landscape (Day 6). You may want to have a guest speaker for this day or do some background research about your topic.

Finally, Wigglin' Worms (Days 13, 14) will require access to earthworms. You may be able to borrow some from a teacher or parent with a worm bin, or you might purchase night crawlers at stores that sell fishing supplies. You might even want to start a class worm bin as a separate project. If you don't have access to a worm bin, start collecting worms at the beginning of the project. You can offer students extra credit points if they bring in worms. If worms are in short supply, you can modify the lesson and measure cricket behavior (e.g., how much crickets move or sing under different environmental conditions). You can purchase crickets at many pet stores.

Planning for the Final Celebration

The final celebration is an opportunity for students to show off all their hard work. Plan the final presentation well in advance so families have plenty of notice. You may need to reserve a special room to have enough space for all the parents and students. The gym, theater, or cafeteria works well. Send out notices to parents at the beginning of the project and reminder slips as the presentation date gets closer. Make it clear to the students and the parents that the students need to be at the final celebration if at all possible. The presentations are difficult to organize when there are students who can't attend. If some students cannot attend, ask parents to notify you early. It is easier for the other group members to work around absentees if they have advance warning. Suddenly missing one presenter out of three or four is tricky to handle. Students may gain more confidence if they have a chance to practice in front of a real audience. It can be fun to invite another class to see the presentations on the day before or the day of the final celebration.

Reference

Black, P., and D. Wiliam. 1998. Inside the Black Box: Raising Standards through Classroom Assessment. *Phi Delta Kappan* (Oct.).

Alignment with *Atlas of Science Literacy* Maps

What should students learn? In what order? And how does each strand of knowledge connect to vital threads? The two illustrations, or "maps," on pages xix–xx help explain how certain skills and concepts fit into the bigger picture of science literacy and science education. The maps, which use the learning goals of the American Association for the Advancement of Science (AAAS)'s *Science for All Americans* (1989) and *Benchmarks for Science Literacy* (1993), are excerpted from *Atlas of Science Literacy*, copublished by AAAS and the National Science Teachers Association (Volume I, AAAS 2001). There are 50 maps in *Atlas of Science Literacy* (and a second volume to come); here we present those titled "Scientific Inquiry: Evidence and Reasoning in Inquiry" and "Scientific Inquiry: Scientific Investigations." Let us examine how *The Truth about Science* curriculum aligns with these two maps.

"SCIENTIFIC INQUIRY: EVIDENCE AND REASONING IN INQUIRY"

According to this map, the sequential and logical development of scientific reasoning skills can be summarized in four parts. First, students learn to make observations and describe them accurately. They also notice that by altering some aspect while continuing to make careful observations, they can learn more (K–2). Second, students learn that if you want to explain how something works, you must have evidence to support your explanation (3–5). Third, science investigations involve making systematic observations to collect evidence that may or may not support hypotheses. This step requires using creative thinking and science reasoning skills (6–8). Fourth, students refine critical thinking and science reasoning skills so that they are equipped to evaluate lines of reasoning and the evidence on which they are based.

The Truth about Science curriculum develops skills and knowledge of scientific reasoning at both the 3–5 and 6–8 grade levels. Thus, it reinforces understandings developed in grades 3–5 and then continues to challenge students to acquire more sophisticated reasoning skills. Upon completion of the curriculum, students will have had experience in all of the four middle-level (6–8) skills and knowledge boxes presented in this map. Further science investigations in the middle school years will continue to reinforce these skills and knowledge until scientific reasoning becomes second nature.

"SCIENTIFIC INQUIRY: SCIENTIFIC INVESTIGATIONS"

As can be seen on this map, the development of skills and knowledge of scientific investigations is similar to that of scientific reasoning in the early grades. Students begin by practicing to make careful and accurate observations (K–2). From these observations, students notice that there is variability in results, even when everything appears to be exactly the same. They learn to keep notebooks where they carefully record how something is set up and what they observed (3–5). Students practice changing one variable at a time and learning how to control other factors (6–8). Finally, students study systems where it is not always possible to observe the effect of one variable. They use evidence and observe as wide a range as possible to find patterns (9–12).

The Truth about Science provides a powerful experience for students to learn all the skills and knowledge boxes in the scientific investigations map. The curriculum reinforces the importance of keeping accurate notes and making careful qualitative and quantitative observations. In The Toughest Towel (Days 11, 12) and Wigglin' Worms (Days 13, 14) lessons, students witness variability in data when they repeat their experiments and compare results. Then they change a variable and repeat the experiment. They can even change two or more variables to discover that they don't know exactly why they got different results. Students learn the importance of replicates and how to interpret data, given natural variability, in the Faux Fish Figuring (Day 25) and Stat Savvy (Day 26) lessons. Conducting the Long-Term Research Project integrates all these skills into a memorable experience in scientific investigation.

References

American Association for the Advancement of Science. 1989. *Science for All Americans*. New York: Oxford University Press.

———. 1993. *Benchmarks for Science Literacy*. New York: Oxford University Press.

———. 2001. *Atlas of Science Literacy*. Arlington, VA: National Science Teachers Association.

Figure i.1. Scientific Inquiry: Evidence and Reasoning in Inquiry

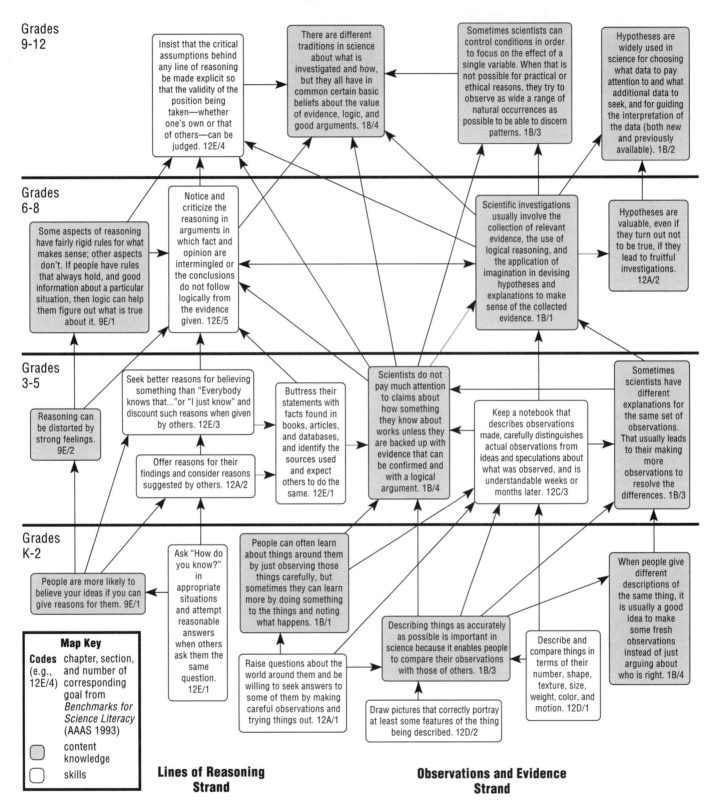

This map was adapted from *Atlas of Scientific Literacy* (AAAS 2001). For more information or to order, go to *www.nsta.org/store*.

Figure i.2. Scientific Inquiry: Scientific Investigations

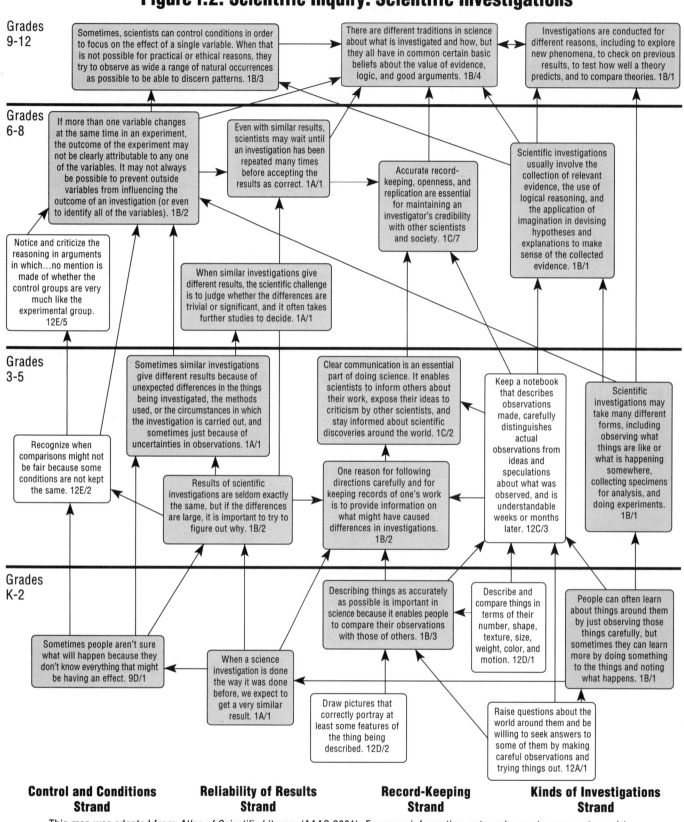

Grades 9-12

Sometimes, scientists can control conditions in order to focus on the effect of a single variable. When that is not possible for practical or ethical reasons, they try to observe as wide a range of natural occurrences as possible to be able to discern patterns. 1B/3

There are different traditions in science about what is investigated and how, but they all have in common certain basic beliefs about the value of evidence, logic, and good arguments. 1B/4

Investigations are conducted for different reasons, including to explore new phenomena, to check on previous results, to test how well a theory predicts, and to compare theories. 1B/1

Grades 6-8

If more than one variable changes at the same time in an experiment, the outcome of the experiment may not be clearly attributable to any one of the variables. It may not always be possible to prevent outside variables from influencing the outcome of an investigation (or even to identify all of the variables). 1B/2

Even with similar results, scientists may wait until an investigation has been repeated many times before accepting the results as correct. 1A/1

Accurate record-keeping, openness, and replication are essential for maintaining an investigator's credibility with other scientists and society. 1C/7

Scientific investigations usually involve the collection of relevant evidence, the use of logical reasoning, and the application of imagination in devising hypotheses and explanations to make sense of the collected evidence. 1B/1

Notice and criticize the reasoning in arguments in which...no mention is made of whether the control groups are very much like the experimental group. 12E/5

When similar investigations give different results, the scientific challenge is to judge whether the differences are trivial or significant, and it often takes further studies to decide. 1A/1

Grades 3-5

Sometimes similar investigations give different results because of unexpected differences in the things being investigated, the methods used, or the circumstances in which the investigation is carried out, and sometimes just because of uncertainties in observations. 1A/1

Clear communication is an essential part of doing science. It enables scientists to inform others about their work, expose their ideas to criticism by other scientists, and stay informed about scientific discoveries around the world. 1C/2

Keep a notebook that describes observations made, carefully distinguishes actual observations from ideas and speculations about what was observed, and is understandable weeks or months later. 12C/3

Scientific investigations may take many different forms, including observing what things are like or what is happening somewhere, collecting specimens for analysis, and doing experiments. 1B/1

Recognize when comparisons might not be fair because some conditions are not kept the same. 12E/2

Results of scientific investigations are seldom exactly the same, but if the differences are large, it is important to try to figure out why. 1B/2

One reason for following directions carefully and for keeping records of one's work is to provide information on what might have caused differences in investigations. 1B/2

Grades K-2

Sometimes people aren't sure what will happen because they don't know everything that might be having an effect. 9D/1

When a science investigation is done the way it was done before, we expect to get a very similar result. 1A/1

Describing things as accurately as possible is important in science because it enables people to compare their observations with those of others. 1B/3

Describe and compare things in terms of their number, shape, texture, size, weight, color, and motion. 12D/1

People can often learn about things around them by just observing those things carefully, but sometimes they can learn more by doing something to the things and noting what happens. 1B/1

Draw pictures that correctly portray at least some features of the thing being described. 12D/2

Raise questions about the world around them and be willing to seek answers to some of them by making careful observations and trying things out. 12A/1

| Control and Conditions Strand | Reliability of Results Strand | Record-Keeping Strand | Kinds of Investigations Strand |

This map was adapted from *Atlas of Scientific Literacy* (AAAS 2001). For more information or to order, go to *www.nsta.org/store*.

Correlations with the *National Science Education Standards*

Training students to be scientists is a logical way to meet many of the *National Science Education Standards* (National Research Council 1996). Fundamental abilities necessary for a student to do scientific inquiry include the ability to

■ identify questions that can be answered through scientific investigations;

■ design and conduct a scientific investigation;

■ use appropriate tools and techniques to gather, analyze, and interpret data;

■ develop descriptions, explanations, predictions, and models using evidence;

■ think critically and logically to make the relationships between evidence and explanations;

■ recognize and analyze alternative explanations and predictions;

■ communicate scientific procedures and explanations;

■ use mathematics in all aspects of scientific inquiry. (National Research Council 1996, 145, 148)

While many published middle school science curricula include laboratory investigations that answer a research question, they rarely provide an opportunity for students to ask their own research questions and to design and carry out appropriate experiments for answering these questions. The skills used to follow a scripted laboratory investigation are much different from those used to formulate a testable research question and to develop corresponding hypotheses and experimental methods. *The Truth about Science* curriculum uses laboratory investigations to teach principles of science research such as control and treatment types, replication, controlling outside factors to limit their influence, randomization, and keeping careful records. Students apply these principles when they design and carry out their own research projects.

Principles of data analysis included in the science standards state that students should develop the ability to use appropriate tools and techniques to analyze and interpret data. The curriculum presented here approaches data analysis from a statistical perspective. Students learn to summarize and represent their data using averages, tables, and graphs. Students learn how to assess and display variance, and they explore how variability in data influences interpretation of that data. These methods push students to think analytically and critically about their data and the overall project. The students must synthesize what they have learned about experimental design and data analysis with the results of their research to interpret and explain their research results.

Reference

National Research Council. 1996. *National Science Education Standards*. Washington, DC: National Academy Press.

Correlations with the *National Science Education Standards**

STANDARD	Days 1, 2, 3 OOZE LESSONS	Days 4, 5 SCIENCE BOXES	Day 6 LOCAL LANDSCAPE	Days 7–10 LONG-TERM RESEARCH PROJECT	Days 11, 12 TOUGHEST TOWEL	Days 13, 14 WIGGLIN' WORMS
Develop descriptions, explanations, predictions, and models using evidence.	■		■	■	■	■
Think critically and logically to make the relationships and models using between evidence and explanations.	■			■	■	■
Communicate scientific procedures and explanations.	■			■	■	■
Use mathematics in all aspects of scientific inquiry.	■			■	■	■
Identify questions that can be answered through scientific investigations.		■	■	■	■	■
Design and conduct a scientific investigation.					■	■
Use appropriate tools and techniques to gather, analyze, and interpret data.					■	■
Recognize and analyze alternative explanations and predictions.					■	■

*National Research Council, 1996. *National Science Education Standards*. Washington, DC: National Academy Press.

National Science Teachers Association

| Days 15–21 | Day 22 | Days 23, 24 | Day 25 | Day 26 | Days 27–40 |
LONG-TERM RESEARCH PROJECT	AQUEOUS AVERAGES	GRAPHING DATA	FAUX FISH FIGURING	STAT SAVVY	LONG-TERM RESEARCH PROJECT
■		■	■	■	■
■	■	■	■	■	■
■					■
■	■	■	■	■	■
■					■
■					■
■		■	■	■	■
■		■		■	■

xxiv

Materials List

- 3-ring notebook for each student
- computer disk for each group
- poster board for each group

Section I: Research Questions and Hypotheses

Day 1—Ooze Observations

- 1 large flat-bottomed bowl or container per student group (shallow containers such as dish buckets work better than deep containers such as regular buckets)
- 1 box of cornstarch per student group
- 1 extra box of cornstarch
- lots of newspapers to cover desks
- masking tape
- food coloring (optional)
- water
- clean-up materials (paper towels, sponge, bucket, broom)
- assortment of "measuring" equipment: e.g., silverware, strainers, yogurt lids, paper towels, toothpicks, measuring cups, stopwatches, funnels, scale, weights, plastic bags

Day 2—Imagining and Planning Ooze Experiments

Day 3—Ooze Experiments

- same as Day 1

Days 4, 5—Science Boxes

- 1 science box per group of students

  Science boxes are theme boxes that can be put together in any type of container (e.g., large envelopes, shoe boxes, plastic tubs, paper boxes). The theme needs to be obvious from the outside of the container either by attaching pictures or labeling with a title. The boxes are filled with items and/or pictures related to the theme of the box. The contents need to lead students to think about different comparisons and quantitative measurements that could be made within that system. See pages 18–20 for examples of the contents of different science boxes.

Day 6—Long-Term Research Project (LTRP): Local Landscape

- Variable; see page 26 for possibilities

Day 7—LTRP: Field Techniques

- Variable; see pages 31–34 for possibilities

Day 8—LTRP: Research Questions and Hypotheses

Day 9—LTRP: Library Research I

- access to library
- access to Internet

Day 10—LTRP: Introduction Paragraph

- access to computer lab
- 1 computer disk for each LTRP group

Section II: Experimental Design

Days 11, 12—The Toughest Towel

- overhead transparency of picture of ring stand setup (page 65)
- 1 ring stand per student group
- 3 or 4 binder clips per group
- water
- paper towels—3–5 different brands. The results are much easier to keep track of if brands have dramatically different color patterns.
- standardized weights—for example, large heavy washers. All weights should be the same and should have no sharp edges. You will need enough weights so that each group can have enough to break through a wet paper towel. (This may need to be tested beforehand.) We recommend 5/8" zinc, cut washers, available at hardware and building supply stores.
- 1 large box or shallow plastic bucket per group (optional)

Days 13, 14—Wigglin' Worms

- 2 identical containers per student group (large yogurt containers or 2 L soda bottles with the tops cut off work well)
- 6 worms per student group
- dirt (enough to fill all the containers at least 3/4 full)
- extra buckets or other containers to put "used" dirt in (1 per group)
- masking tape
- water
- metric rulers
- large spoons
- newspapers

- a few lights
- portable heater or other heat source

Day 15—The Wheel of Inquiry Game!

- 2 dice
- chalkboard or overhead to display the secret phrase, used letters, vowels, and score
- prizes (optional)

Days 16, 17—LTRP: Methods and Materials

- access to computer lab
- map of field site
- box or bag for each student group to keep its materials together

Day 18—LTRP: Data Sheets

- overhead transparencies of Sample Data Sheets
- graph paper with light lines
- rulers
- Rite in the Rain paper (optional, available through scientific supply stores and bookstores)

Days 19, 20—LTRP: Field Trips

- overhead transparencies of Sample Data Sheets
- clipboards and pencils for each student group
- each group will require different materials and will have identified and gathered them on Days 16, 17
- camera with film
- parent volunteers

Section III: Summarizing and Analyzing Results

Day 21—LTRP: Tables Tell the Tale

- 1 ruler for each student
- 1 sheet of graph paper for each student

Day 22—Aqueous Averages

- 6 tall, clear plastic cups or graduated cylinders per student group
- food coloring
- water
- newspapers
- paper towels

- 1 tray
- 1 pitcher
- colored markers (optional)
- calculators

Days 23, 24—LTRP: Graphing Data

- light-colored butcher paper
- dark markers
- 1 copy each of Graphs 1, 2, 3 per student group (provided on pages 114–116)
- overhead transparencies of Graphs 1, 2, 3
- 6–10 overhead transparencies, blank or with graph-paper lines copied onto them
- 1 ruler for each pair of students
- several sheets of graph paper for each pair of students
- computer access and disks if students are to do computer graphing of LTRP data

Day 25—Faux Fish Figuring

- 1 envelope per student pair
- 1 pair of scissors per student pair
- butcher paper or overhead transparencies to display class graphs

Day 26—Stat Savvy

Day 27—T-Test Practice

- calculators

Day 28—LTRP: T-Tests

- calculators

Day 29—LTRP: Results Paragraph

Day 30—LTRP: Library Research II

- access to library
- access to Internet

Days 31, 32—LTRP: Discussion Paragraph

- access to computer lab

Section IV: Presentation of Research Projects

Day 33—LTRP: Peer Reviews

- copies of every group's research report (introduction, methods, results, discussion—without names)

Days 34, 35, 36—LTRP: Poster Preparation

- 1 poster board per group (color requests may be possible if orders are taken in advance)
- blank paper, graph paper, colored paper
- markers, pens, pencils
- scissors, paper cutter, ruler, glue sticks
- pictures from field trips, if available
- field samples (small branches, fern fronds, etc.) for decorating posters (The field samples should be pressed or covered with clear contact paper.)

Days 37, 38, 39—LTRP: Preparing Research Presentations

- overhead transparencies (about 8 per research group)
- permanent markers
- index cards
- access to a copy machine
- Appendix C: Worm Presentation copied onto transparencies

Day 40—LTRP: Practicing Research Presentations

- overhead projector
- screen
- pointer (optional)

LTRP: Celebration Night

- place for presentations
- overhead projector
- screen
- microphone
- extension cord
- pointer (optional)
- food and beverages (optional)
- printed program
- award certificates

The Truth about Science brings you *sci*LINKS, a new project that blends the two main delivery systems for curriculum—books and telecommunications—into a dynamic new educational tool for students, teachers, and parents. By linking specific science content with instructionally rich Internet resources, *sci*LINKS creates new pathways for learners, new opportunities for professional growth among teachers, and new modes of engagement for parents.

In this *sci*LINKed text, you will find an icon near several of the concepts you are studying. Under it, you will find the *sci*LINKS URL *www.scilinks.org* and a code. Go to the *sci*LINKS website, sign in, type the code from your text, and you will receive a list of URLs that are selected by science educators. Sites are chosen for accurate and age-appropriate content and good pedagogy. The underlying database changes constantly, eliminating dead or revised sites or simply replacing them with better selections. The ink may dry on the page, but the science it describes will always be fresh. *sci*LINKS also ensures that the online content teachers count on remains available for the life of this text. The *sci*LINKS search team regularly reviews the materials to which this text points—revising the URLs as needed or replacing webpages that have disappeared with new pages. When you send your students to *sci*LINKS to use a code from this text, you can always count on good content being available.

The selection process involves four review stages:

1. First, a cadre of undergraduate science education majors searches the World Wide Web for interesting science resources. The undergraduates submit about 500 sites a week for consideration.

2. Next, packets of these webpages are organized and sent to teacher-webwatchers with expertise in given fields and grade levels. The teacher-webwatchers can also submit webpages that they have found on their own. The teachers pick the jewels from this selection and correlate them to the *National Science Education Standards*. These pages are submitted to the *sci*LINKS database.

3. Scientists review these correlated sites for accuracy.

4. NSTA staff approve the webpages and edit the information provided for accuracy and consistent style.

*sci*LINKS is a free service for textbook and supplemental resource users, but obviously someone must pay for it. Participating publishers pay a fee to NSTA for each book that contains *sci*LINKS. The program is also supported by a grant from the National Aeronautics and Space Administration (NASA).

RESEARCH — QUESTIONS AND HYPOTHESES

Background Information

The lessons in this section introduce students to the process of scientific investigation, define the vocabulary of scientific research, and develop skills in asking testable research questions.

In the first three lessons on Ooze (Days 1, 2, 3), students explore the creative side of scientific research. Ooze, a mixture of cornstarch and water, can appear to be a liquid or a solid. If you move it slowly, it pours and drips. If you hit it, rub it, or roll it into a ball, it appears to be a solid. At first, students will simply focus on making observations: qualitative and quantitative. Then, students will design their own one-day experiments about Ooze and learn the four parts of a scientific report or presentation: introduction, methods, results, and discussion.

SCiLINKS.
THE WORLD'S A CLICK AWAY

Topic: scientific method
Go to: www.sciLINKS.org
Code: TAS01

The Science Boxes lesson (Days 4, 5) explores the differences between information and research questions and pushes students to ask their own research questions about many different natural systems. In the next lessons (Days 6, 7) students learn about their Long-Term Research Project (LTRP) site and a variety of techniques for studying trees, plants, insects, birds, water quality, and climate, if they will be doing field-based projects. Teachers who direct students to do lab-based projects can use this time to introduce students to different lab techniques and equipment. With this background, students will be ready to ask interesting, testable research questions.

The final three lessons (Days 8, 9, 10) initiate the LTRP. Each student group will define its research question and hypotheses and conduct background research at the library. In the final lesson, students draft an introduction paragraph for their poster presentation.

The following concepts will be important for the lessons in this section. The concepts are presented in the general order in which they will be presented to the class.

Qualitative and Quantitative Observations

Qualitative observations describe the qualities of an object. Quantitative observations describe the quantity of something. An easy distinction for students to remember is that quantitative observations can be summarized with a number while qualitative observations cannot. Because they use numbers, quantitative observations can be precisely and objectively compared.

The following are examples of qualitative observations: *A leaf is green. A leaf is dark green. A leaf is bumpy. A leaf has veins. A leaf has a lot of veins. A chair is hard. A flower smells good. A flower is stinky.* These qualitative descriptions can be compared but not precisely. You can say, "This flower smells good, but this flower is stinky." But how much more stinky is it? A quantitative observation has a precise number attached to it: *The flower has seven petals. The leaf has 34 veins. The car weighs 1.2 tons. The dog blinked 37 times in one minute. The chicken took 34 seconds to cross the road.* These quantitative observations can be compared precisely and objectively.

Some things are easier to quantify than others. Time, length, and weight are easy to quantify, but smell, taste, and attitudes are very difficult. Researchers often have to find innovative methods for summarizing qualitative observations in a quantitative way—for example, *Seven people thought the flower was smelly while four people could not smell anything.* These numbers can be compared. You could then ask whether more people think a daisy is smelly or whether more people think a rose is smelly. You didn't quantify the smelliness but you created an alternate measure. You could quantify smelliness with a rating—for example, a scale of 1 to 5, with 1 being the most pleasant and 5 being the least.

The best rule of thumb for deciding if something is qualitative or quantitative is to ask if you can summarize the information in a number. This is, however, only a rule of thumb; occasionally a qualitative observation can have a number in it—for example, *That smells like five-day-old cornbread.* A quantitative observation is a measurement of something. A qualitative observation is a description of something.

The reason we care about quantitative observations versus qualitative observations is that quantitative observations tend to be more objective (though not always), more precise, and much easier to compare. The LTRPs will depend on quantitative observations. Students may also record qualitative observations to help them remember certain conditions or observations that don't lend themselves to quantitative measures.

Four Parts of a Scientific Report

Scientists have a standard method for writing up research results. The format is used for scientific papers, posters, and oral presentations. A report is usually divided into four sections, and they are always presented in the same order. (Later, when the media report on science findings, this structure is lost. A report in *Newsweek* or on the nightly news is not the same as a scientific report.)

The first section is the *introduction*. The purpose of the introduction is to introduce the reader to the subject and to the research question in the context of what is already known. Usually an introduction includes a little bit of general information on the topic, provides any specific information that might be necessary to understand the context of the question, and states what other researchers have already learned about the topic. If you have a theory of what you expect to find, you can state it in the introduction. For example, the introduction section might include a sentence such as, "Birds forage for insects in the bark of tall trees, so we expect to find more birds in trees than on the ground." The introduction should make the project sound so exciting that someone will want to read the rest of the report. The introduction always states the research question and the hypothesis being tested. The purpose of an introduction is *not* to introduce the researchers themselves but rather to introduce the issue being studied.

The second section is the *methods*. The methods are a set of directions for conducting the research. The methods section has two purposes. First, it should be clear enough that the reader understands exactly what was done and can evaluate the techniques used. For example, a reader might be interested in whether the results are simply due to the time of day at which the measurements were taken or to the type of equipment used. All those details should be in the methods section. The second purpose is to provide enough information that others could repeat the experiment exactly and see if they get the same results. In ecological research, the methods section often includes a site description. The site description gives a general description of the area—location, vegetation in the area, local weather patterns, and any other details relevant to the research question. A map is a fun thing to add to the site description.

The *results* section is the third part of the research report and is usually the easiest to write. It simply describes the results of the research. Almost always, the results section includes a table and/or a graph describing the data that were collected. The text of the results section describes the table and the graph, pointing out important details. The text might identify any unusual data points and describe the variability in the data. The results of statistical analyses go in the results section after the data description.

The fourth section is the *discussion*, which describes why you think the data showed particular patterns. Has anyone else found similar results? Do your results confirm your original theory or are they surprising? Often, scientists will build a new theory from their data and describe it in the discussion section. Other things to include in the discussion are things that could have affected your results (thermometers may not have been accurate enough to measure subtle differences in temperature), things you would change if you were to do it again (collect more data, control for rain, do the research in the summer), and ideas for research projects that build on these results. A great topic for the discussion section is the implication of the research results. For example, if you found that a stream had very low pH, you could recommend some changes to pollution laws.

Information Questions versus Research Questions

An information question is designed to gather a broad spectrum of information on a topic. For example, "How do birds fly?" and "Why is it colder in winter?" are information questions. One research project cannot answer an information question; a large amount of study will be required.

Research questions that guide science research set up a specific comparison that can be tested. For example, "Do birds fly faster on sunny or rainy days?" and "Is the air temperature colder or warmer than the ground temperature under wet leaves?" are both examples of research questions. It is easy to imagine how measurements could be taken to answer these questions. For the first, you would have to measure flight speeds for lots of birds in different conditions. For the second question, you would need to measure the air and under-wet-leaf temperature in several places.

A helpful key to identifying information versus research questions is that information questions usually start with "why," "how," or "what." Research questions usually begin with "do," "are," or "is." There are lots of exceptions to this rule, but it's a good place to start.

Answers to research questions are the building blocks of scientific theory. Answers to information questions are built on the answers to many research questions all put together.

Hypothesis versus Null Hypothesis

Hypotheses and null hypotheses are a convention of scientific research that is often used to facilitate statistical analysis. Hypotheses are testable predictions. There are lots of different ways to formulate hypotheses, but for the LTRP, we will stick with one standardized method. The LTRP hypothesis states that there is a difference between the two things being compared in the research question. The null hypothesis states that there is no difference between the two things being compared. Together, the hypothesis and the null hypothesis account for all possible outcomes.

For the temperature example, the hypothesis would state that there is a difference between air temperature and under-wet-leaf temperature. The null hypothesis would state that there is no difference between air temperature and under-wet-leaf temperature. Notice that the hypothesis does not state which location you think will be warmer or colder, simply that there will be a difference. We have categorized all possible outcomes into two statements. No matter what results we find, we will be able to choose one statement or the other.

When doing research, we assume that the null hypothesis is true and we set out to see if we can disprove it. This may not make much sense at first, but there is a good reason for doing it this way. It is much easier to prove something is not true (the null hypothesis) than to prove that something is true. In Section III: Summarizing and Analyzing Results, we use statistical tests to decide whether the data provide enough evidence to reject the assumption that the null hypothesis is true.

The important things for students to understand at this point are (1) we set up all research projects by stating the hypothesis and the null hypothesis, (2) we start out by assuming that the null hypothesis is true, and (3) we gain information about whether the hypothesis or the null hypothesis is true by gathering data.

Ooze Observations — Day 1

Overview

In this lesson, students practice making observations, the most fundamental skill in conducting scientific research and one that they will have to perform for their Long-Term Research Projects (LTRPs). Scientists make two types of observations: qualitative and quantitative. Qualitative observations describe how something looks, feels, behaves, or smells, using *adjectives*. Quantitative observations describe something with *numbers*. This lesson uses Ooze, a mixture of cornstarch and water, as a medium for making both qualitative and quantitative observations.

Focus Question
What is the difference between qualitative and quantitative observations?

Science Skills
■ Students should be able to make and record qualitative observations.

■ Students should be able to make and record quantitative observations.

Background
For background information on the concepts in this lesson, see "Qualitative and Quantitative Observations" (page 1).

Materials
■ 1 large flat-bottomed bowl or container per student group (shallow containers such as dish buckets work better than deep containers such as regular buckets)

■ 1 box of cornstarch per student group

■ 1 extra box of cornstarch

■ lots of newspaper to cover desks

■ masking tape

■ food coloring (optional)

■ water

■ clean-up materials (paper towels, sponge, bucket, broom) *Ooze cannot be poured down the drain.*

- assortment of "measuring" equipment: e.g., silverware, strainers, yogurt lids, paper towels, toothpicks, measuring cups, stopwatches, funnels, scale, weights, plastic bags

- Ooze Observations Worksheet (provided)

Development of Lesson

PREPARATION:

The teacher can prepare the room and the Ooze beforehand to save time or students can cover their desks and mix the Ooze during the lesson.

- Worktables can be covered with newspaper. This will work best if held in place with masking tape so it doesn't slip off.

- Ooze is just cornstarch and water (see the Ooze recipe on page 15). A few drops of food coloring can be added to the water for a little extra pizazz. The proportions are approximately 1 1/2 to 2 cups of water to 1 box of cornstarch. Add the water slowly, mixing the cornstarch by hand, until it has reached Ooze consistency. It is Ooze when it flows easily in the bowl when tilted and it appears solid when hit or rubbed on the surface. Add a little extra cornstarch if it gets too soupy. The mixture will solidify as the kids handle it, so it is better to err on the slightly soupy side than to start with the mixture too solid.

WHEN THE STUDENTS ARE READY TO BEGIN:

1. Divide the students into groups of four to six students at each work station. Each group should designate a recorder. For the second half of the class, a new recorder will be designated so everyone has a chance to play with the Ooze.

2. Explain to them that they are going to make observations about a very unusual substance. One of the first people to describe this substance was Albert Einstein in 1906 (Sneider 1993). Ask about the difference between quantitative and qualitative observations. It may help students to use the words *quantity* and *quality* to start. For group practice, students can make qualitative observations about the room, a poster, a person, or an odd object and then make quantitative observations about the same item. Solicit enough examples to convince you that the students understand the basic differences.

3. Set up a few ground rules for Ooze. No throwing. No tasting. Ooze should remain over the table at all times (i.e., no carrying or holding over the floor). It should never be more than 1 foot above the table. *Tell students that they must not dispose of Ooze down the drain.* Students should wipe hands and equipment with paper towels before cleaning in sink.

4. If the Ooze and room have been prepared ahead, quickly remix each pot of Ooze and deliver it to the tables. Otherwise, have the students prepare the room and Ooze as described under Preparation above.

5. Give the students a few minutes to explore the Ooze.

6. Hand out an Ooze Observations Worksheet to each group and ask each group to write down a list of five qualitative observations about the Ooze. You may have to circulate from table to table to keep the process going as it will be difficult to stop and start the class once the Ooze is on the table. Give students five minutes or so to make their qualitative observations.

7. Now ask the students, in groups, to write down five quantitative observations about the Ooze. This will be hard! Ask them to brainstorm about some of the things that they could measure. It might help to show them the available measuring equipment (see Materials, above). Students will have a difficult time making quantitative observations about Ooze, and they will probably need a lot of input and ideas from you. To some degree, the equipment you provide will push their thinking. Some examples of things to measure are as follows: time for a ball to melt into a puddle, time for a certain volume to run through your fingers, time for a certain volume to run through a funnel, amount of weight that can be stacked on top of a yogurt lid before it starts to sink, weight of Ooze that can be picked up with a fork, weight that can be picked up with a spoon, number of spoonfuls that can fit in another container, search time to locate sunken objects, weight of a certain volume of Ooze, weight or volume of Ooze that can sit on a paper towel before it breaks, height at which something can be dropped on the Ooze and not splash, or volume of Ooze that can fit in a plastic bag.

8. Circulate from group to group handing out the measuring equipment. Each group should be able to use a few pieces of equipment. Passing equipment between groups will get messy.

9. After the students have had about 10 minutes to make their quantitative observations, initiate the cleanup.

10. Have students record the group observations on their own worksheets and put them in their three-ring binders for later reference. (Teachers might want to photocopy the group observations, rather than have students copy them by hand.)

11. **Extra.** Have the students imagine a fancy machine for making a quantitative measurement about Ooze. How would it work? What would it measure? Students can draw, diagram, and explain their measurement devices. Some ideas are a boxing glove on a spring that delivers a punch with an exact force; a cup on a pivot tray that tilts very slowly at an angle; or a mechanical nose that can measure smell.

Discussion Questions

1. Are qualitative or quantitative observations easier? Why? What kinds of things are easy to measure qualitatively? Quantitatively?

2. How can you tell if something is a qualitative or a quantitative observation? Can an observation be both?

3. How could you make a chart of qualitative observations? Could you graph them? How? What about quantitative observations?

4. Why might scientists rely on quantitative versus qualitative observations?

5. How could you take a qualitative observation and make it quantitative? Can you think of an example? *He is tall. He is 5 feet tall. Roses have a strong smell. On a scale of 1 to 10, the strength of a rose smell is an 8 or 9.*

6. If you were going to conduct an experiment and you were going to repeat it over and over to make sure you got the same results each time, would you want to be recording qualitative or quantitative observations? Why? Why might you want to repeat the experiment over and over?

REFERENCES

The following references provide valuable information about Ooze, also commonly referred to as Oobleck. The book by Sneider has a host of other fun projects to extend the lessons on Ooze, and the two articles in *Scientific American* provide interesting information about its physical chemistry. The Dr. Seuss book is an enjoyable and relevant story.

Kerr, P. F. 1963. Quick Clay. *Scientific American* 209(5): 132-42.

Sneider, C. I. 1993. *Oobleck: What Do Scientists Do?—Teacher's Guide*. Berkeley, CA: Lawrence Hall of Science, University of California.

Seuss, Dr. 1949. *Bartholomew and the Oobleck*. New York: Random House.

Walker, J. 1978. The Amateur Scientist: Serious Fun with Polyox, Silly Putty, Slime, and Other Non-Newtonian Fluids. *Scientific American* 239(5): 186-98.

Ooze Observations Worksheet

QUALITATIVE OBSERVATIONS:

1. _____

2. _____

3. _____

4. _____

5. _____

QUANTITATIVE OBSERVATIONS:

1. _____

2. _____

3. _____

4. _____

5. _____

IMAGINING AND PLANNING OOZE EXPERIMENTS

Overview

In this lesson, students explore the creative side of science while learning the fundamental issues in research design: planning, safety, making and recording observations, and drawing conclusions. As students design their own experiments with Ooze, they are introduced to the four components of a scientific report. The four components will constitute the basis for their Long-Term Research Projects (LTRPs).

Focus Question

What are the four components of a scientific report?

Science Skills

- Students should be able to ask questions that can be answered by doing a small-scale experiment.

- Students should be able to state the four parts of a scientific report.

Background

For background information on the concepts in this lesson, see "Qualitative and Quantitative Observations" (page 1); "Four Parts of a Scientific Report" (page 2); and "Treatment Types" (page 53).

Materials

- Ooze Experiment Worksheet (provided)

Development of Lesson

1. Begin with a class discussion about observations and Ooze. Have the students share their qualitative and quantitative observations from the previous lesson. Can the students determine rules for differentiating between qualitative and quantitative observations?

2. As a group, discuss the question "What are the steps that a scientist must consider when doing scientific research?" The group discussion should move toward the fol-

lowing conclusions: Research is used to answer a question; research must be planned; all the details have to be specified in advance, including safety precautions; research is made up of a series of observations (usually quantitative); the observations must be recorded systematically; you use these observations to draw a conclusion about your original question.

3. Take a few minutes to discuss several safety issues that may become important while doing science research projects. First, students should never taste science materials. Even though Ooze is just cornstarch and water, it has had lots of hands in it and is in tubs that might have contained other, unknown materials. Second, floor spills can create slippery areas and should be wiped up immediately. Third, care should be taken that chemicals, including Ooze, don't get into someone's eyes. Where are goggles stored and when do they need to be used? Does the classroom have an eyewash station available? Finally, remind students that roughhousing and throwing materials are not appropriate behaviors for scientists in the laboratory/classroom.

4. Students break into the same small groups that explored Ooze together. Ask them to brainstorm a list of questions about Ooze. It may help to keep track of their ideas on a piece of scratch paper. Once they have at least five questions, ask them to imagine experiments that would provide the answers to these questions. These questions and experiments can be both reasonable and ridiculous.

5. After students have time to generate some creative ideas, announce that tomorrow each group will actually be able to do an experiment with Ooze on their own. The only requirement is that the experiment include some sort of quantitative observation. Their task for the rest of the lesson is to design an experiment on Ooze that they can complete in one hour with materials in the classroom or that they bring from home. Some parts of the experiment can be done at home in advance if students wish (e.g., "What happens when Ooze dries overnight?").

6. The concepts of treatment types and replication can be introduced here if the teacher feels that the students are ready. These ideas are formally introduced in Section II: Experimental Design (pages 53–57). For some classes, it works well to have the students thinking ahead to the important details of experimental design when they design these small experiments. For other classes, there is enough new material and it is better to leave treatment types and replication for later lessons.

7. Students will be writing a scientific report about their Ooze experiments. Have the students discuss what should be in a scientific report. A scientific report should answer several questions: (1) Why was the experiment done? (2) What exact steps did the experiment include? (3) What are the results? (4) What can be learned from the experiment? Ask the students why the answers to these questions are important. What kind of information will they need to answer each one of the questions? What other questions might be answered in a scientific report? Introduce the four parts of a scientific report: introduction, methods, results, and discussion (see pages 2–3, "Four Parts of a Scientific Report"). Which question is answered in each section? What kinds of information go in each section?

8. Have the students work together in their small groups to choose one Ooze experiment that can be completed in a class period. As each group tells you its idea, hand out one Ooze Experiment Worksheet to each group member. Students should fill in the first two sections on the Worksheet: introduction and methods. Each student should write out a detailed description of the proposed methods for the group experiment, including the materials required, safety precautions, steps to be carried out, and observations to be recorded (some observations must be quantitative). Methods can be continued on a separate sheet of paper if required.

The teacher will have to circulate among groups to make sure that everyone has something simple and feasible. If students are stuck, the following make interesting experiments: What happens if you add water? Milk? Salt? Soda pop? Flour? Sugar? What happens if you bake it? Let it dry out? Microwave it? Freeze it in bags? Freeze it in ice cube trays? Let it thaw out again? How long will it stick to something? How long does it take to go through a funnel? Different sizes of funnels? Could you paint with it? What does newsprint do to it? Can it pick up pictures like Silly Putty can?

9. If there is time, students can share their favorite questions and wacky experiment ideas as a class and/or they can share their experimental design for the next day and other groups can provide suggestions.

10. This is a good time to introduce (with lots of enthusiasm!) the overall structure of *The Truth about Science* curriculum. Explain to students what types of activities they will be doing in class and describe the Long-Term Research Project (LTRP). Let them know that they will have a chance to ask their own research questions and collect their own data. They will be scientists! The next 10 weeks will involve learning and practicing the process of scientific research, spending time collecting data, graphing and analyzing data, and presenting results as a poster and as an oral presentation.

11. Remind students to bring in any materials or preparations that they will need for the next day. If they need to make Ooze at home to start the experiment, a recipe is provided on page 15 that can be copied and circulated. Ooze should not go down the drain at home either!

Discussion Questions

1. What makes a scientific experiment different from just trying different stuff?

2. Why do you need to plan all the details of an experiment? *In science, it is important that an experiment be repeatable. This way, researchers can test whether what happened was just a fluke or they can identify which step caused which result.*

3. Why might a scientist want to repeat someone else's experiment?

4. What other steps and ideas do you think will be important in doing scientific research?

5. What is the hardest part about making an experimental plan or design?

6. What are the four parts of a scientific report and what information goes in each part?

National Science Teachers Association

Ooze Experiment Worksheet

INTRODUCTION:

To *introduce* your experiment, explain any details about Ooze that you think someone might need to know to understand or be interested in your experiment. You can use some of your qualitative and quantitative observations from the first day.

_____

_____

_____

_____

WHAT QUESTION ARE YOU TRYING TO ANSWER?

_____

_____

_____

METHODS:

What *methods* will you use? Describe your experimental plan and any modifications that you made while actually conducting the experiment. It might help to write the plan as a series of steps.

_____

_____

_____

_____

_____

_____

RESULTS:

What happened when you did your experiment? What were the *results*?

_____

_____

_____

DISCUSSION:

What do you conclude about Ooze? Write a brief *discussion* of what you discovered from your experiment.

_____

_____

_____

_____

_____

_____

_____

_____

Ooze Recipe

You will need:

- 1 large mixing bowl
- 1 spoon
- 1 box cornstarch
- 1–2 cups of water
- food coloring (optional)

Pour most of the box of cornstarch into the bowl (save a little for adjustments). Add about 1 1/2 cups of water and several drops of food coloring. Stir in all the cornstarch. It will cake at the bottom of the bowl, but this needs to get mixed in too. It's usually easier to use your hands than just the spoon. The Ooze should be the consistency of pancake batter. If it is too thick, add more water. If it's too thin, add the extra cornstarch.

Dispose of Ooze in the garbage, not down the drain!

Ooze Recipe

You will need:

- 1 large mixing bowl
- 1 spoon
- 1 box cornstarch
- 1–2 cups of water
- food coloring (optional)

Pour most of the box of cornstarch into the bowl (save a little for adjustments). Add about 1 1/2 cups of water and several drops of food coloring. Stir in all the cornstarch. It will cake at the bottom of the bowl, but this needs to get mixed in too. It's usually easier to use your hands than just the spoon. The Ooze should be the consistency of pancake batter. If it is too thick, add more water. If it's too thin, add the extra cornstarch.

Dispose of Ooze in the garbage, not down the drain!

Day 3 ———————— OOZE EXPERIMENTS

Overview

In this lesson, students carry out Ooze experiments according to the experimental methods that were written during Imagining and Planning Ooze Experiments (Day 2). Students must follow their original plans carefully, noting any changes that must be made. Each group should make at least one type of quantitative observation. Through this process, students become familiar with the structure of scientific report writing as demanded by their Long-Term Research Projects (LTRPs).

Focus Question

How do you report the results of scientific research?

Science Skills

- Students should be able to follow a proposed experimental design.
- Students should be able to make observations and draw conclusions from them.
- Students should be able to describe the type of information in each of the four components of a scientific report.

Background

For background information on the concepts in this lesson, see "Qualitative and Quantitative Observations" (page 1); "Four Parts of a Scientific Report" (page 2); "Treatment Types" (page 53); and "Replication" (page 54).

Materials

- 1 large flat-bottomed bowl or container per student group (Shallow containers such as dish pans work best.)
- 1 box of cornstarch per student group
- 1 extra box of cornstarch
- lots of newspaper to cover desks
- masking tape
- food coloring (optional)
- water

- clean-up materials (paper towels, sponge, bucket) (Ooze cannot be poured down the drain.)
- assortment of "measuring" equipment: e.g., silverware, yogurt lids, paper towels, toothpicks, measuring cups, stopwatches, funnels, scale, weights, plastic bags
- Worksheet from Day 2 (Ooze Experiment Worksheet)

Students may also have materials from home for their independent projects.

Development of Lesson

1. Prepare the room for a big mess. Worktables can be covered with newspaper and held in place with masking tape.

2. Have the students make the Ooze and carry out their research plan. It should be stressed that they need to follow their original plan. If they need to make changes, they should make careful records of those changes.

3. As each group finishes, they need to clean up their area and equipment. No Ooze down the drain!

4. Each person should finish his or her Ooze Experiment Worksheet, reporting results and discussing conclusions.

5. Meet as a group and share the results of the experiments. Review the four parts of reporting an experiment: introduction (including the research question), methods, results, and discussion. Have each group describe its quantitative observation.

6. If there is time, you might want to introduce the concepts of treatment types and replication. Define the concepts and ask students how controls, alternative treatments, and/or replication might have been useful for their experiments. These concepts will be formally introduced in Section II: Experimental Design.

Discussion Questions

1. What things did you have to change in your experimental design? Why?

2. What was the hardest part of designing the research project?

3. Was it easier to come up with qualitative or quantitative observations? Why?

4. Do you think you would get the same results if you repeated the experiment over and over?

5. What information would be missing if you left out one section of the experimental report (introduction, methods, results, discussion)?

6. What is the difference between results and discussion?

Overview

Topic: ecosystems
Go to: www.sciLINKS.org
Code: TAS18

Students practice formulating testable research questions, hypotheses, and null hypotheses by examining the contents of "science boxes" filled with things related to a particular ecosystem or science theme. Using the contents of the boxes to inspire thinking, students formulate research questions that compare two things and are specific, measurable, and repeatable. A testable research question will easily suggest a hypothesis (there is a difference between two things) and a null hypothesis (there is no difference between two things). Students play a game using the science boxes, trying to come up with as many different and unique testable research questions as possible. On Day 8, students will formulate testable research questions for their Long-Term Research Projects (LTRPs).

Focus Question

What is a testable comparison research question?

Science Skills

■ Students should be able to define and state a testable research question, hypothesis, and null hypothesis.

Background

For background information on the concepts in this lesson, see "Information Questions versus Research Questions" (page 3); "Hypothesis versus Null Hypothesis" (page 4); and "Qualitative and Quantitative Observations" (page 1).

Materials

■ 1 science box per student group

Science boxes are theme boxes that can be put together in any type of container (e.g., large envelopes, shoe boxes, plastic tubs, paper boxes). The theme needs to be obvious from the outside of the container either by attaching pictures representing the theme or giving the box a title. The boxes are filled with items and/or pictures related to the theme of the box. The contents need to lead students to think about different comparisons and quantitative measurements that could be made within that system. Following are a few ideas:

Beach Box: beach grass, fine and coarse sand, crab backs, large and small shells, driftwood, sea bird feathers, beach pictures, thermometer, pictures of barnacles on wood or shells, high tide and low tide pictures, different types of seaweed, driftwood, shorebird pictures.

River/Stream Box: preserved aquatic insects, live insects in a plastic box, sediment samples, pH paper, cattails, willow branches, aquatic insect field guide, pictures of river fish (e.g., salmon, trout, sturgeon), small net, large and small river rocks.

Forest Box: pine cones, branches, different types of soil, pine needles, leaves from other forest plants, bark, forest insects, pictures of wild mushrooms, book of animal tracks, thermometer, tree field guide.

Bird Box: bird books, different types of birdseed, bird feeders, feathers, birdhouse, bird nest, tape player with tape of bird calls, pictures of birds in different habitats.

School Yard Box: birdseed, insects, plant seeds, fertilizer, soil types, weeds, grasses, different types of birdhouses or bird feeders, thermometer.

Flight Box: paper airplanes, balsa airplanes, kites, bird pictures, balloons (air pressure), rockets, toy bats, spring balance, string, straw, loopers, butterfly wings, feathers, model insects, helicopter toy (roll in hands and it flies).

Motion Box: tops, gears, pulley, teeter-totter, different size and weight balls, tape measure, stopwatch, spring balance, wheels, sandpaper, marbles, lubricating oil, ramps, pendulum, roller skate, pictures of sled/skis/toboggan, toy cars and trucks, in-line skates, skateboard, bicycle parts.

Electricity Box: batteries, magnets, paper clips, compass, wires, alligator clips, light bulbs, holiday lights wired in series, balloon (static electricity), plastic comb, felt, Styrofoam ball, Ping-Pong ball, Styrofoam beads, dynamo (bike light generator), copper strip, aluminum strip, lemon, voltmeter.

Light Box: prism, light source, colored paper, thermometer, colored cellophane, mirrors, spectroscopes, different types of light, different colors of light bulb, 3-D glasses, book of optical illusions, strobe flashlight, sundial, light meter, plant seeds, tinfoil.

Sound Box: string and two cups, test tubes with different levels of water, rubber bands stretched between nails on a board, wooden ruler, paper megaphone, mystery shaker with various noisemakers inside, drum, balloons, bat pictures, dog whistle, bells, cups, different liquids, AM and AM/FM radios, tuning forks.

Matter and Energy Box: liquids of different densities, oil and vinegar mixture, solids, gas, balloons, recycled materials, rusty nail, shiny nail, baking powder and vinegar, pH paper, oil and colored water in two different types of bottle.

Weather Box: thermometer, rain gauge, pinwheel, balloons, water sample, soil sample, sundial, bubbles, windsock, sun paper, sunscreen, compass, weather maps, different types of insulation, barometer (homemade and/or store bought), different fabrics (Gortex, plastic, down-filled).

Rocks, Minerals, and Geology Box: scale, graduated cylinder, petrified wood, household objects made out of rock, geodes, rock identification book, geology book, geological maps of region and area, magnifying glass, magnet, streak plate, Mohs' hardness scale to test hardness, glass hardness tester, bottle labeled "acid," rocks from the garden, rocks from the beach, rocks from the river, zinc oxide.

Astronomy Box: star chart, telescope, magnifying glass, meteorites, book on constellations, dark glasses, flashlight and balls of different sizes (to simulate orbits and eclipses), different types of sundials, half sphere and small suction cup with stick (to track sun movement across the sky).

Waves Box: metal slinkies of different sizes, plastic slinkies, springs, liquids of different viscosity in tubes or bottles, flashlight, radio, X-ray, sheets of plastic of different thicknesses, sand, pictures of waves, toy surfboard, toy boats, bubble bath, walkie-talkies.

■ Science Boxes Worksheet (provided; each group will need one Worksheet for each box)

Development of Lesson

1. Have the students close their eyes and imagine they are at the beach, in the forest, at a pond, looking at an airplane, or testing a light bulb. What do they see? What do they hear? What do they smell? What do they find interesting?

2. Ask the students for qualitative and quantitative observations based on what they have imagined.

3. Select one box as a demonstration. Go through the contents with the class. Have the students ask "why," "what," and "how" questions about anything that interests them in the box. Tell them that these are examples of information questions.

4. Have the students select two items from the box (or two things they imagine would be at the real place) that could be compared. Have the students formulate questions about the comparison. These will generally be questions that begin with "do," "are," or "is." For example, are sand crabs more active during the day or at night? Examine the information questions and the comparison questions with the class. Which type of question leads to doing a science experiment? Why? *Comparison questions suggest a difference that can be tested experimentally between two things.*

    Beach box is selected. Teacher shows class fine sand and coarse sand, shells of different shapes and sizes, crab claws and exoskeletons, pictures of barnacles on a piling, high tide and low tide pictures, different types of seaweed, driftwood, shorebird pictures. Teacher: "What different 'why' and 'how' questions can you ask about the items in the box?" Students: "Why do crabs lose their shells? How do barnacles attach to wood or shells? Why does the tide change?" Teacher: "Now name some of the different things at the beach that could be compared." Students: "Large and small crab claws; high tide and low tide water levels; shorebirds at high tide and low tide; mussel and clam shells; Puget Sound beach and Pacific Ocean beach." Teacher: "Try to state each one of the comparisons as a question. If you're having trouble, use questions that begin with 'do,' 'is,' or 'are.'" Students: "Do large crabs and small crabs use the same area of the beach? Does the distribution of mussel shells and clamshells differ? Are there more shorebirds present at high tide or low tide? Is there a difference between high and low tide water levels from day to day? Do Puget Sound beaches have more trash than Pacific Ocean beaches?" Teacher: "Which questions—information or comparison questions—suggest a science experiment that you could do?"

5. Introduce to students the concepts of hypothesis and null hypothesis. Although many science curricula teach the hypothesis to be an educated guess, in our case it is a general statement that there is a difference between two things. For the crab example, the hypothesis is "There is a difference in sand crab activity during the day and during the night." Null comes from the French word *nul*, meaning "not any" or "not." The null hypothesis states "There is no difference in sand crab activity between day and night." If the students want to make an educated guess, they can make a prediction and should call it that rather than a hypothesis to avoid confusion. Have the students state research questions, hypotheses, and null hypotheses until they are confident with the terms and what they mean.

6. Now the fun begins. Once the students have shown that they grasp the idea of comparison research questions, hypotheses, and null hypotheses, you can begin the science box game. Divide the students into as many groups as you have boxes. We suggest a minimum of six groups so groups have no more than five members. Make sure that groups include a mix of student abilities to make them academically similar. Each group has one of the science boxes. Before starting, tell the students that the game is a contest to see which group can come up with the most research questions that are different from any other group's questions. Give the groups five minutes to write down as many different comparison research questions as they can. If they run out of room on the front of the worksheet, they can use the back. After five minutes, the groups rotate to the next box. (Or the boxes can rotate to the next student group.) Begin again. Have a different group member record the questions that the group generates at each box.

7. Groups need one Science Box Worksheet per box. (You can put as many Worksheets as there are groups in each box or you can give each group one Worksheet per box.) Once the game is over, each group member can have one of the Worksheets to keep in his or her science notebook. If there are at least as many boxes as there are group members, then each group member can keep the Worksheet that he or she recorded. Most likely, you will not complete the rotation of groups and boxes on the first day. Begin the second day by continuing the observation of science boxes until every group has seen every box.

8. Once each group has generated questions for every box, put the science boxes away and reassemble the class. Compare the questions that each group came up with for each box. First, make sure all the questions are comparison research questions. If they aren't, they don't count. Second, any questions that more than one group came up with don't count. Cross these questions off the list. Third, have each group state a hypothesis and null hypothesis for each question remaining on its list. Each group gets a point for every research question and hypothesis that no other group came up with. The group with the most points wins. Prizes are up to the teacher.

Discussion Questions

1. How are information questions different from comparison questions?

2. Why are comparison questions more useful for doing science research than information questions?

3. What does it mean to ask a question that is testable? What are the different criteria that make a question testable?

4. Is there a limit to the number of comparison research questions that can be asked? Why or why not?

5. Is it difficult to ask a good testable research question? Why or why not?

6. Come up with several research questions about a new topic (e.g., social science, medicine, marketing).

Homework

The homework assignment (see Comparison Research Questions Worksheet, page 24) reinforces the idea of a testable comparison research question and allows the students to take the next step in designing their own experiments to try to answer the question.

Worksheet

Name _____ Page # _____

Science Boxes Worksheet

Group Names _____

Box Theme _____

COMPARISON RESEARCH QUESTIONS:

1. _____
   _____

2. _____
   _____

3. _____
   _____

4. _____
   _____

5. _____
   _____

6. _____
   _____

7. _____
   _____

8. _____
   _____

Be prepared to state a **hypothesis** (there is a difference between…) and a **null hypothesis** (there is no difference between …) for each research question!

Comparison Research Questions Worksheet

1. Name two things that you could compare.

_____and_____

2. Write a comparison research question about the two things.

_____

_____

3. State a hypothesis and a null hypothesis for your research question.

hypothesis:

`_____

_____

null hypothesis:

_____

_____

4. Describe an experiment you could do to try to find an answer to your question.

_____

_____

_____

_____

5. What qualities make a good research question?

_____

_____

_____

_____

LONG-TERM RESEARCH PROJECT (LTRP): LOCAL LANDSCAPE

Day 6

Overview

The objective of this lesson is to prepare students to ask research questions that can be answered during the Long-Term Research Project (LTRP). For many classes, the preparation involves introducing students to the local ecology of the area in which they will be conducting their research. For classes focusing on Earth and physical science or classes not planning to gather field data, the lesson can be used to introduce important background information. Students should come away from this lesson with a list of interesting comparisons that could be used to set up research questions for the LTRP and a list of things that could be measured quantitatively. As students learn details about the LTRP site, local vegetation, local animals, history, and climate patterns, they will be better able to ask interesting and engaging research questions. If students will be conducting their LTRP with an Earth or physical science focus, this period should be used to introduce students to enough general material that they can ask interesting questions. The lesson plan offers several variations because requirements and resources will be different for every class. Before the lesson begins, the teacher needs to have selected and visited the exact site for the LTRP. This lesson involves more independent preparation by the teacher than any other lesson. It is helpful to read the lesson plan for LTRP: Research Questions and Hypotheses (Day 8) before preparing this lesson.

Focus Question

What research comparisons and quantitative observations could be studied during the Long-Term Research Project (LTRP)?

Science Skills

- Students should be able to list at least three comparisons that could be investigated for the LTRP.

- Students should be able to identify at least three things for the LTRP that could be measured quantitatively.

Background

For background information on the concepts in this lesson, see "Selecting the LTRP Site and Planning for Data Collection" (page xv); "Lessons That Require Advance Planning" (xv); "Qualitative and Quantitative Observations" (page 1); and "Information Questions versus Research Questions" (page 3).

Materials

The materials required for this lesson will depend on the LTRP topic and the chosen approach. Some possibilities include the following:

■ slide projector and slides of the LTRP site

■ manipulatives for learning about Earth or physical science

■ samples of items found at the LTRP site: pinecones, leaves, etc.

■ books or LTRP topic-specific resources

■ audiovisual equipment for a guest speaker

■ small plastic bags and scavenger hunt list

Development of Lesson

BEFORE THE LESSON:

1. **a.** If a field trip is planned, the teacher should choose and visit the LTRP site before this lesson. While at the site, think about potential comparisons for the LTRP and which things could be measured quantitatively. Some suggestions are listed below; further ideas are provided in LTRP: Field Techniques (Day 7). Locate as much information about the LTRP site and the local ecology as possible. If the site is a park, the city, county, or state park department may have information. Local libraries and conservation groups will also have information about native plants, important ecological drivers of the local environment (e.g., amount of rainfall or soil pH), local history (Was the site once a landfill? Was there ever a fire?), local bird and insect species, and interrelationships among the environment, plants, birds, and insects.

    b. If the LTRP will not be focused on ecology, this lesson should be used to provide experience with concepts that can be examined experimentally. For example, the lesson might be used to describe fundamentals of aviation for a class planning to focus their LTRPs on topics having to do with flight, or to describe fundamentals of cloud formation, wind, and precipitation patterns for a class planning to conduct research on weather-related topics. Students should be able to generate research questions from the ideas and concepts presented. No matter the topic, the focus of this lesson should be on identifying interesting comparisons and quantitative measures in the LTRP topic area. If the teacher is unfamiliar with the topic, this is a good lesson to invite a guest presenter.

2. Choose one of the four approaches discussed below (field trip, guest speaker, slide

show, discussion) that will work best for your class. The approach that provides the most interesting information will be the most effective one. As students learn details and begin to ask questions about the LTRP topic, they will become more engaged in their project and they will be able to ask more thoughtful research questions.

THE LESSON:

3. For all of the approaches, begin with a review of the important attributes of a testable research question. A testable research question should compare two things using quantitative observations.

4. Review the general structure of the LTRP with the students. They should be aware that they will have the opportunity to develop their own research questions and to collect their own data.

5. Tell the students that the day will be used to help them learn about the LTRP site or topic and to help them get ready to decide on their LTRP research question.

6. Initiate the lesson: the field trip, the guest speaker, the slide show, or the discussion.

7. Have the class come up with a list of good comparisons and quantitative observations for the LTRP topic. A list could be made on the board or students could write their own lists. It will be helpful if the students have access to this list in later lessons.

8. Finally, have students brainstorm a list of safety issues related to their topics. If the class plans to collect data in the school yard, there might be a few safety concerns. If the class is going on a field trip, they might want to discuss having partners, road safety, noxious plants, or water safety. Put the emphasis on the students' ability to maintain a safe environment for themselves and not on all the possible disasters that could occur. Classes planning indoor experiments should discuss traditional lab safety.

LESSON APPROACHES:

Field Trip. Visit the LTRP site with the class and look for interesting comparisons. Any information about the site history, soil conditions, local plants, or common insects that you can provide will help the students to identify interesting comparisons. This approach will work best if the LTRP site is the school yard or a neighboring park. Challenge the students to identify things that can be compared and things that can be measured. Students could work in teams to come up with lists of comparisons or quantitative measures. A more directed approach might be to give each team a small plastic bag and a scavenger hunt list. Have the students collect items that suggest comparisons and/or quantitative measures. Items might include a sketch of a bug found on a conifer tree and of a bug found on a deciduous tree, the circumference of one deciduous and one coniferous tree, soil from near the building and soil from under the shrubs, a leaf with insect damage and a leaf without damage, the height of two different types of grass, a leaf from a shrub and a leaf from a tree, cones from two different types of trees, the temperature of standing water (supply thermometers in bag), the temperature of soil at the surface and 5 cm below the surface, the temperature of soil in the sun and the shade, or seeds from two different types of plants. Items on the list can be organized, as above, to suggest specific comparisons, or they can be organized randomly so that students must identify potential comparisons. After the scavenger hunt, meet as a group and create a list of potential comparisons and quantitative measures.

Guest Speaker. Invite a local expert to give a presentation about the LTRP topic, the LTRP site, and/or important local ecological processes. The guest speaker will need to be comfortable giving presentations to this age group, and he or she will need to be briefed on the purpose of the presentation. The goal of the presentation is for the students to explore interesting comparisons and potential quantitative observations. Guest speakers will probably not be able to give their standard talks, but most local experts will be able to modify their standard talks to focus on the details students will need to write their own LTRP research question. Potential guest speakers can be identified through local universities; local conservation groups; city, county, or state parks; and natural resources departments.

Slide Show. Take pictures of things that would make interesting comparisons. Develop the pictures as slides and present a slide show about the LTRP topic emphasizing a few key concepts (e.g., "patterns of sun and shade influence plant communities" or "waves have both a frequency and an amplitude that may vary"). The slide show can be organized around interesting comparisons and potential quantitative observations. This approach is fairly labor intensive as background reading will also be required, but the materials can be used again in future years. Include as much student interaction and discussion as possible.

Discussion. Lead a class discussion about the LTRP topic. What is found at the site? What is interesting about the topic? What are the important scientific principles? Objects can be used to motivate the discussion and to suggest interesting comparisons. This approach will work well if the students have already spent time studying the LTRP topic and/or if they are familiar with the LTRP site (e.g., if the site is the school yard or a nearby park). This approach will also require a good deal of background reading. At the end of the discussion, students should be able to identify some interesting comparisons and potential quantitative observations at their LTRP site.

COMMON COMPARISONS FOR FIELD PROJECTS:

These comparisons can be used at many sites. Some may not be appropriate for certain LTRP sites. Many others can be added.

- sun versus shade
- wet versus dry soil
- northern versus southern exposures
- near buildings versus far from buildings
- deciduous versus coniferous trees
- shrubs versus trees
- grassy areas versus dirt

■ near water versus far from water

In school yards, students may elect to modify the environment. In this case, they could base comparisons around the following:

■ two brands of birdseed

■ two types of insect traps

■ yellow light versus white light

■ the natural environment versus a treatment (e.g., watering, pruning, weeding, adding nontoxic fertilizer, shading)

COMMON QUANTITATIVE MEASURES:

■ tree height or width or density

■ plant density

■ number or species composition of insects, flowers, or plants

■ soil or water pH

■ temperature

For further ideas, see the list of potential research questions for LTRP: Research Questions and Hypotheses (Day 8) and Science Boxes (Days 4, 5).

Discussion Questions

1. Name two things that you could compare for your LTRP. Why is it an interesting comparison? What makes you think that there might be a difference between them?

2. What makes your LTRP site unique?

3. What kinds of things could you study at the LTRP site?

4. Name two things that you could measure quantitatively in your LTRP topic area.

5. How are observations different from experiments? What different types of issues do you have to think about when planning the project? *Observations usually involve comparing two things and controlling for unwanted influences. Experiments usually require a treatment and a control.*

Day 7 —————————— LTRP:
FIELD TECHNIQUES

Overview

This lesson introduces students to techniques used by scientists to measure and quantify various aspects of the natural environment. It must be done outside, where students can practice using the techniques. The teacher must be able to demonstrate the techniques or find someone who can (e.g., county extension person, university graduate student in forestry, botany, or biology, or a teacher who has used the curriculum). The techniques described here present basic concepts and methods for quantifying field observations, but many other techniques exist. Students should be encouraged to develop and modify techniques to answer their specific research questions. *Note:* Use this lesson to introduce laboratory techniques if your long-term research projects (LTRPs) will not be field-based.

Focus Question

How can different environmental conditions be measured?

Science Skills

■ Students should be able to perform several techniques that can produce quantitative data.

■ Students should be able to determine whether a technique produces quantitative or qualitative data.

Background

For background information on the concepts in this lesson, see "Selecting the LTRP Site and Planning for Data Collection" (page xv); "Qualitative versus Quantitative Observations" (page 1); and "Repeatable" (page 55).

Materials

Depends on which field techniques the teacher uses. Here are a few ideas:

■ *Forests:* tape measures, plant/mushroom field guides, plant press, magnifying lenses, precipitation gauges, plant/tree field guides

■ *Invertebrates:* hanging sticky traps, trowels, clipboards, white paper, clear contact paper

■ *Animals:* binoculars, bird field guides, stopwatch, track plates

■ *Stream/lake:* thermometers, small nets, white trays, aquatic insect field guide, wide-mouthed water bottles, water testing kit

■ *Soil:* thermometers, trowels, zip-type plastic sandwich bags, or yogurt containers

Development of Lesson

Field techniques must be taught and learned outdoors. Listed below are different standard field techniques that can be easily learned and used by students. You may choose to demonstrate three or four techniques to the entire class or print the instructions and have the students use them as an instruction manual. Other options include contacting a county employee or a university graduate student familiar with these techniques and having them demonstrate techniques to the students. The bottom line is that these techniques are standardized and repeatable in different conditions. If a group wants to compare the number of mushrooms growing in the forest versus the number growing in open fields, they must count mushrooms in plots of exactly the same size in both locations for the comparison to be valid.

If you are familiar with the techniques that will be demonstrated, then you may also want to introduce students to the concept of randomizing observations. This concept is discussed in more detail in Section II: Experimental Design.

TERRESTRIAL VEGETATION TECHNIQUES

1. **Vegetation Transects**. To quantify the number of plants or different species of plants, botanists and foresters often use vegetation transects. Stretch a tape measure out a predetermined distance (e.g., 10 m). You have just created a transect. At each 1 m interval, observe and then quantify the number or types of plants found along the tape. This can be done in a number of different ways:

   a. Decide which is the dominant plant species covering the first meter of the transect. Record the name. A meter may be dominated by, for example, a log, stump, tree, stream, bare soil, or mushrooms. Record only one dominant plant for every interval. Once you have finished all 10 meters, add the percentages for any plants that are dominant in more than one interval.

   b. Simply count the number of a certain kind of plant found along the transect. For example, in 10 m, there may be 12 sword fern plants.

   c. List or count all the different species or kinds of plants along a transect. This method quantifies the species composition (e.g., 12 species along transect A versus 2 species along transect B).

2. **Vegetation Quadrats**. This is another method for quantifying vegetation or ground conditions. Instead of using a transect, a "quadrat" or fixed area is determined and delineated. For example, a common quadrat size for examining small plants or mushrooms is 1 m square. Students can take a length of twine, string, or lightweight rope, measure out 4 m and tie a knot at each meter. The twine can be laid out on the ground with the knots at each corner. Place a stick or stake to hold each corner in place. (Using pre-measured ropes reduces the number of tape measures that are needed

in the field.) Once the quadrat has been laid out, different methods can be used to quantify whatever you are interested in within the quadrat:

a. Count the number of, for example, mushrooms, rocks, spiders or other invertebrates, ferns, wood sorrel, or seedling trees in the quadrat. This is the number found per square meter.

b. Measure the total area covered by, for example, moss, bare soil, logs, rocks, or water within the quadrat. This is the area per square meter. The area can be expressed either as the area or as a percentage.

c. Use larger quadrats to quantify larger features such as trees. A 10 m × 10 m quadrat can be measured and all the trees identified and counted within the quadrat.

3. *Tree Diameters*. The size of trees can be measured using a tape measure and some basic geometry. Measure 1.5 m from the ground on the high side of a tree if it is on a hill. Then measure around the tree at this point. This is a measure of circumference. To convert to diameter, divide the circumference by pi (3.14159).

TERRESTRIAL INVERTEBRATE TECHNIQUES

1. *Ground Invertebrates*. Invertebrates or "bugs" provide a much more reliable source of data than other animals. Students who are interested in studying animals should be encouraged to focus on invertebrates. Students can count the individuals found within a small quadrat (1 m × 1 m; see Vegetation Quadrats above). The overall number of invertebrates, the number of different species, the number of one specific species, or the number of one type of invertebrate (e.g., spiders, insects, centipedes, millipedes, slugs) can be recorded.

2. *Branch Beating for Invertebrates.* Entomologists often use a technique called "branch beating" to compare invertebrates in different kinds of trees or in different locations. The investigator selects a reachable branch and shakes it for a predetermined length of time or number of shakes onto a piece of white paper or a piece of contact paper, sticky side up. (It works well to clip a piece of contact paper on a clipboard, sticky side up, shake the branch, and then cover the sticky part with the wax paper. Make observations from the clear side of the contact paper.) The number of invertebrates shaken from the branch is counted. Different species or types of invertebrates (caterpillars, aphids, other flying insects) can be identified and recorded. A hand lens is useful for examining very small specimens. Specimens can also be placed in alcohol vials and taken to the classroom for further examination.

3. *Insect Traps*. Hanging flytraps or sticky traps can be placed in different kinds of trees or in different locations and left overnight. If the sticky surface is exposed, cover the surface with clear contact paper when collecting the traps. The insects are then identified and counted. This can be done back in the classroom or outdoors. Hanging flytraps are available at hardware and grocery stores.

4. *Investigation of Leaf Damage.* Aphids as well as other insects eat deciduous leaves. The presence of the insects can be detected by examining leaves for damage. Students examine a predetermined number of leaves from a tree and count the number

of damaged/eaten leaves versus undamaged leaves. In the fall, students may have to pick up the leaves from the ground.

5. **Soil Invertebrates.** Measure a small area on the surface of the ground. Dig a hole of this size to a predetermined depth. Place the dirt you remove on a piece of white plastic (kitchen garbage bag or white bucket). Sort through the dirt and remove any invertebrates. Record the species or type of invertebrate and the number of invertebrates for each hole.

VERTEBRATE TECHNIQUES

1. **Bird Census.** Using a field guide and a pair of binoculars, identify and count birds found in a predetermined area. Comparisons can be made of the number of different species, the number of one species, or the total number of birds. Make comparisons based on different environments, different times of day, or different weather conditions. If male and female individuals can be identified, students can compare time spent in different behaviors by individuals of different sexes.

2. **Small Mammal Tracks.** Mammal tracks can be observed in muddy areas along streams, rivers, and lakes. Students can use animal-track field guides to identify the tracks and compare the number of species observed at different areas. If you take plaster of Paris along, students can make casts of the tracks. Track plates are another way to survey animal activity in an area. The plates can be made with cookie sheets or other sturdy surfaces that can be blackened from candle or alcohol burner soot. Place track plates with sooted side up in different areas (field and forest, near water and far from water, under shrubs and in the open) flush with the ground so the animal does not have to climb up over the edge of the plate. Plates must be balanced so they don't jiggle and scare animals that start to walk on them. To protect track plates from rain and falling leaves, cover them with cardboard boxes. Cut two sides off the boxes for animal entrances and cover with plastic so boxes don't get soggy and collapse on the plates.

AQUATIC TECHNIQUES

1. **Water Temperatures.** Use an unbreakable thermometer to measure water temperatures at different depths, locations, or different times of day.

2. **Sediment Samples.** Examine the amount of sediment suspended in the water by collecting equal volumes of water in clean, wide-mouthed jars. Take the samples back to class. To separate the suspended sediment from the water, students can pour water samples through filter paper. Take 2 L plastic pop bottles and cut the tops off so they make funnels. Place filter paper in a funnel and place the funnel in the open end of the pop bottle that the funnel was cut from. Slowly pour a set volume of the water sample through the filter paper. Let filter paper with sediment dry. Weigh the filter paper before you start and after drying. Subtract the initial weight from the final weight. This gives you the mass of the suspended sediment for a particular volume of water.

3. **Water Quality Measures.** Aquatic ecologists measure levels of dissolved oxygen, pH, nitrate, ammonia, phosphorous, calcium, salinity, carbon dioxide, chlorine, and

other constituents to determine the amount of water pollution or water quality. Most of these tests are available in kits from the major biological supply houses; some simple kits are available at pet stores that sell fish. Determining the pH of water is one of the easiest tests. Extra time may be needed to explain to the students why it is important to know the pH level and what it means. In an outreach program based at the Seattle Aquarium, employees give classroom presentations or meet a class at a stream, measure water quality, and talk about its effects on animal and plant life in the stream. County natural resources departments employ fieldworkers who regularly measure water quality in lakes and streams in the county. They can be approached for technical assistance.

4. *Water Velocity or Flow.* Place a leaf or stick on the surface of the water and measure the amount of time it takes to travel a predetermined distance.

5. *Aquatic Invertebrates.* Place a large aquarium net with a fine mesh in the water. Scrape the bottom of the stream, pond, or lake by hand within a predetermined area or for a predetermined time. Use the current and your hands to sweep dislodged sediment and invertebrates inside the net. It may be necessary to move rocks, scraping each one by hand, in the area of interest. Empty the net into clean water in a bucket or pan with a white bottom. Identify and count the invertebrates you find. Students can compare invertebrates in fast-moving and slow-moving areas of the stream, in rocky bottoms (substrates) and in sandy substrates, under aquatic plants and on similar substrates without plants.

OTHER IDEAS

1. *Precipitation gauges.* Students can compare the precipitation under a conifer tree, under a deciduous tree, and out in the open.

2. *Air temperatures.* Students can compare air temperatures near bodies of water, in interior forests, and in open fields. There are many more possibilities if students can use thermometers that measure minimum and maximum temperatures over a period of time.

3. *Wind velocities.* Students can use a pinwheel device to measure wind velocities in a field, at the edge of a forest, and at the interior of a forest. Comparisons can also be made between wind over a stream and away from the stream.

Discussion Questions

1. State a research question and describe a sampling technique for answering it that gives quantitative information.

2. Why is it important that each technique generate quantitative observations?

3. Design a different technique from the ones listed above that would generate quantitative observations.

4. Why must sampling techniques be standardized? In other words, if you compare ducks on rainy days versus sunny days and you count the number of birds that alight on a

specific dock for an hour on a sunny afternoon, why must you also sit and watch for an hour on a rainy afternoon?

5. How could you standardize a survey for stream invertebrates if you want to compare the number found near the mouth of the stream (downstream) and near the source of the stream (upstream)?

Day 8 ——————LTRP: RESEARCH QUESTIONS AND HYPOTHESES

Overview

Students form their Long-Term Research Project (LTRP) groups, brainstorm, and agree on a research question and hypotheses. Teacher guidance is essential in this process. Teachers must ensure that research questions are testable and feasible without intruding on the students' ownership of their research projects. The lesson described here presents many different research questions to help the teacher guide students as they develop their own questions. LTRP groups should be determined before beginning this lesson.

Focus Question

What are some different research questions that could be used for LTRPs?

Science Skills

■ Students should be able to brainstorm research questions for which an experiment could be designed and conducted, given limited time and resources.

■ Student research groups should be able to carry out a consensus-forming process to decide on one research question for the group to investigate.

■ Students should be able to state a hypothesis and null hypothesis for their research questions.

Background

For background information on the concepts in this lesson, see "Classroom Organization" (page xiv); "Information Questions versus Research Questions" (page 3); and "Hypothesis versus Null Hypothesis" (page 4).

Materials

■ Research Questions and Hypotheses Worksheet (provided)

Development of Lesson

1. Review with the class the field site that will be used for LTRPs. Will it be a forest, field, wetland, lake, or stream? What types of plant and animal life can students expect to encounter?

2. If in-class experiments will be performed, review the available equipment and the possible range of topics.

3. Brainstorm possible research questions suitable to the field site or topic. Encourage students to think about appropriate measurement techniques. You may need to remind them that research questions need to compare two things.

    Here is a list of possible research questions to help guide students. By reviewing this list, you will be better prepared to give students feedback on their questions. *Do not give the list to students! Have them come up with their own questions.*

LIFE SCIENCE

Plants

- Do more sword ferns grow close to the water or away from the water?

- Do different kinds of plants grow on north- and on south-facing slopes?

- Are understory (ground) plants more dense on north- or on south-facing slopes?

- Do seeds grow faster in sandy soils or in dirt soils?

- Does more moss grow on logs than on live trees?

- Does more moss grow on trees on north- or on south-facing slopes?

- Does more moss grow on the north or on the south side of a tree trunk?

- Do plants watered with tap water grow at the same rate as those watered with rainwater?

Trees

- Do trees grow closer together by the stream or away from the stream?

- Are mature (>30 cm diameter) conifer trees taller than mature deciduous trees?

- Do tree species, tree density, tree diameter, or tree height differ between north- and south-facing slopes?

- Do plants growing underneath deciduous trees differ from plants under coniferous trees?

- Do different amounts of rain reach the ground in open areas, under deciduous trees, and under coniferous trees?

Invertebrates

- Are there more spiders on the ground or in tall bushes?

- Do more ground invertebrates live near the stream or away from the stream?

- Is there a difference in the number of invertebrates in a 10 × 10 cm area in dry soil versus in wet soil?

■ Is there a difference in the number of invertebrates in a 10 cm × 10 cm area in shaded soil (under a bush or tree) versus in unshaded soil?

■ Do more small animals live in forests or in open fields?

■ Do more invertebrates live on and around deciduous or coniferous trees?

■ Do more aphids live on red alders or on big leaf maples?

■ Do more worms live on land than live by water?

■ Are there more ground invertebrates on north- or on south-facing slopes?

■ Do invertebrates under deciduous trees differ from invertebrates under coniferous trees?

■ Do different widths of copper strips prohibit slug passage differently?

Birds

■ Do bird species differ along streams and away from streams?

■ Do male mallards spend more time fighting with other ducks than female mallards? (Are male mallards more aggressive than female mallards?)

■ Do birds sing more from 8:30–9:00 a.m. or from 3:00–3:30 p.m.?

■ Do different types of birdseed attract different species of birds?

■ Do different types of habitat (e.g., coniferous trees, deciduous trees, bushes) attract different species of birds?

Miscellaneous

■ In a park, do trash cans placed next to the parking lot collect more trash than trash cans placed next to a pedestrian entrance, away from the parking lot?

PHYSICAL SCIENCE
Sound

■ Are adults more sensitive to loud sounds than teenagers are?

■ Do plants grow more when exposed to music than when they are never exposed to music?

Light

■ Do plants grow faster when exposed to polarized light or to nonpolarized light?

Magnetism

■ Do plants exposed to a magnetic field bloom more frequently than plants not exposed to a magnetic field?

■ Is there a difference in the strength of an electromagnet when there are 70 wire coils around a bolt or 100 wire coils?

■ Is there a difference in the strength of an electromagnet when the core is 1/4" diameter steel or 1/2" diameter steel?

Changes of State

■ Does water evaporate faster when it is in the sun or when it has a fan on it?

■ Does water in a can wrapped in black construction paper become hotter than water in a same-sized can wrapped in white construction paper?

■ Does water or soil heat faster in the sun?

■ Does freshwater or saltwater heat faster in the sun?

■ Are liquids at room temperature more dense than the same liquids heated 10°C above room temperature?

Motion and Forces

■ Does it take more force to pull objects over coarse sandpaper than over fine sandpaper?

■ Do balls with 20 lbs psi bounce higher than balls with 15 lbs psi?

Consumer Issues

■ Do Brand A or Brand B batteries last longer? (any two brands will work)

■ Can Brand A plastic wrap hold more weight than Brand B?

■ Do greasy dishes soaked in Brand A dishwashing detergent have less grease remaining than those soaked in Brand B?

■ Does Brand A stain remover remove more of a stain than does Brand B?

■ Do Brand A paper towels absorb more liquid than does Brand B?

■ Is glue stick glue stronger than liquid glue?

Miscellaneous

■ Do beeswax candles burn faster than regular wax candles of the same size?

■ Do beeswax candles heat water to a higher temperature than regular wax candles?

■ Can an egg oriented in a vertical direction hold more weight than an egg placed in a horizontal direction?

■ Does a paper airplane made from heavier paper fly farther than one made from lighter paper?

EARTH SCIENCE

Soil

■ Are soil temperatures on the south sides of buildings higher than those on the north sides?

■ Are soil temperatures in areas where water collects higher than soil temperatures in areas that are well-drained?

Water Quality

■ Is there more acid (lower pH) in the lake or in the stream?

■ Are streams colder than lakes?

- Are there more particulates in the water at the top of the stream, at the bottom of the stream, or in the lake?

- Do stream temperatures differ between forested and nonforested streams?

- Do stream invertebrates differ between forested and nonforested streams?

- Does sediment in stream water differ above a road and below a road?

- Do sandy soils have a higher pH than clay soils?

- Does the water quality (pH, clarity, phosphates, dissolved oxygen (DO), nitrates, sediment, temperature) of water flowing into a lake at the mouth of a stream differ from the water quality in the middle of the lake?

- Is there a difference in the water quality (pH, clarity, phosphates, DO, nitrates, sediment) of melted snow and that of rain?

4. Assign students to research groups of three to five students. These are the LTRP groups for the remainder of the curriculum.

5. LTRP groups complete the Research Questions and Hypotheses Worksheet, brainstorming research questions in their topic. Students must agree on one research question, write the hypothesis, and write the null hypothesis. The teacher can circulate between groups, asking and answering questions to guide groups in this process.

6. At the end of the worksheet, there is a line for the teacher to initialize the final research question, hypothesis, and null hypothesis.

7. Time permitting, the LTRP groups can share their research questions and ideas with the class at the end of the period.

Discussion Questions

1. What criteria can you use to decide whether or not you have come up with a good research question?

2. What background knowledge or information helped you think of different research questions?

3. How does the scientific method combine both creative and critical thinking skills?

4. What difficulties might you run into while investigating (doing the experiment for) your research question?

5. How can you quantify your observations to answer the research question?

Research Questions and Hypotheses Worksheet

GROUP MEMBERS

_____

1. What topic has your group decided to study? _____

_____

2. Write down as many different comparison research questions for this topic as you can think of. Here are some different types of comparisons to help you get started. There are lots more so don't be afraid to come up with new ideas.

northern and southern exposures	near and far from water (lake or stream)
shady areas and sunny areas	near and far from buildings
on the lawn and under trees	on logs and on the ground
on the lawn and under logs	wet soil and dry soil
sandy soil and garden soil	under coniferous and under deciduous trees

_____

_____

_____

_____

_____

_____

3. As a group, choose one of the research questions for your project. Everyone in the group must agree with the choice. Write the question below.

Research Question: _____

_____

_____

4. Write the hypothesis (that states there is a difference between the two things) and the null hypothesis (that states there is no difference between the two things) below.

Hypothesis:

_____

_____

_____

Null Hypothesis:

_____

_____

_____

5. Write your prediction—that is, what you think the answer to your research question will be—and why you think this.

_____

_____

_____

6. What kind of information could you find out about this research question from books in the library?

_____

_____

_____

Teacher Approval: _____

Congratulations!
**You've chosen your research question and can get ready
to begin the project!**

LTRP: LIBRARY RESEARCH I

Day 9

Overview

This lesson is the first of two library visits (the second visit occurs on Day 30). The goal of this first visit is for students to gather background information about their topic before they begin their actual data collection. At the library, students will improve their general understanding of the topic and see how their research fits into the general body of knowledge called science. For the most part, it will be very difficult if not impossible for students to find direct answers to their research questions. This is good; they have conceived research questions that will further the understanding of our natural world. Students begin the lesson by identifying what they already know about the topic. Then they make a topic web to help identify keywords (subtopics) that relate to the topic of their research question. Each student selects one keyword and finds at least one source of information relative to the research question. Students will read and take notes on the topic from this source. Collectively, each group will review the information gathered by every member and use this to help write the introductory paragraph (Day 10).

Focus Question

What can we learn from library resources about our LTRP research question?

Science Skills

- Students should be able to identify what they already know about their selected topic.

- Students should be able to select keywords and find books or webpages that contain relevant background information about the research question.

- Students will be able to take notes from the source on general information regarding the research question.

- Students will be able to start a bibliography of relevant sources.

Background

For background information on the concepts in this lesson, see "Information Questions versus Research Questions" (page 3) and "Four Parts of a Scientific Report" (page 2).

Materials

- access to library

- access to Internet (optional)

- Library Research I Worksheet (provided)

Development of Lesson

1. *Note*: If students have had very little experience doing library research, teachers may want to consider beginning the research in the classroom with selected reference materials available on a cart. This ensures the most efficient use of class time, without students becoming lost in their search for reference materials. You may also want to team with the language arts teacher and the librarian to introduce students to library research. If the library does not have a strong collection of books related to student topics, you may want to provide additional reference materials from public or university libraries.

2. Begin the discussion by reviewing the difference between information questions and research questions. How are they different? Where can you find answers to information questions? What kinds of sources provide an overview or general information about a topic? Why do scientists search library references before beginning their research projects? You can tell the class that today they will be finding background information on their research topics. Learning more about their topic will help them write an introduction paragraph and develop their experimental methods.

3. Review the importance of keeping a bibliography. Why do research reports always include a bibliography? What is plagiarism? How will starting the bibliography now be useful during later stages of the research project? How are bibliographies written and organized? Use the examples at the end of the Library Research I Worksheet.

4. Review behavior expectations for working in the library, if necessary.

5. To begin their survey of relevant information, students first identify what they already know about their topic (question 2 on the Worksheet). They transform this knowledge into a web of related topics and subtopics. Each of the subtopics serves as a keyword to direct the library search. An example of a topic web is given on page 45. Model the creation of a web for the class. On a blank overhead, recreate the example as you discuss topics related to the research question "Is there a difference in the kinds of invertebrates found in soils under deciduous and coniferous trees?" Once the students have identified the subtopics, they use these as keywords to begin the search. If each student finds, reads, and takes notes from one good reference on his or her topic, the group should have enough information to write the introduction paragraph.

6. When using the Internet, direct students to a few good sites or search engines you are familiar with. A lot of time can be wasted doing multiple searches and sifting through layers of pages before finding the relevant page. You can direct students to *www.nrcse.washington.edu/truth/student/studentlist.asp* for sites suggested by other teachers.

Discussion Questions

1. What does your group know already about your research topic?

2. What other information would help you understand the research better?

3. How is an information question different from a research question?

4. Why do scientists always include library research in their work? How do they give other authors credit for their ideas?

5. How much is already understood about our world? How much is there left to find out or discover?

6. Scientists must keep their data as organized as librarians keep their libraries. Why?

7. Where does the information found in libraries come from? *From research that was done in the past. Answers to many research questions can be combined to answer information questions.*

TOPIC WEB

Research Question

Is There a Difference in the Kinds of Invertebrates Found in Soils under Deciduous and Coniferous Trees?

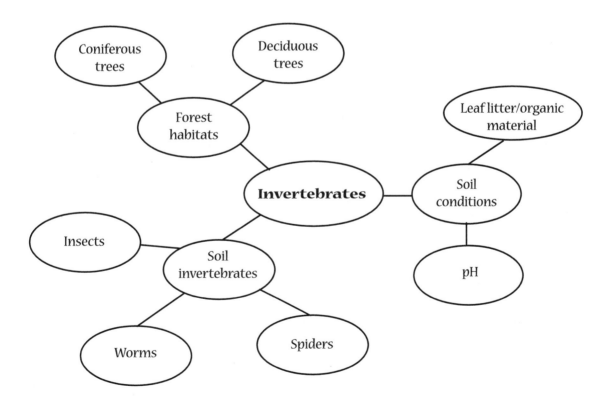

Name _____ Page # _____

Library Research I Worksheet

1. What is your group's research question? _____
_____

2. What do you and your LTRP group already know about your topic? _____
_____
_____
_____
_____
_____

3. Topic web of your research project:

4. Choose one keyword from the web above that you want to learn more about. Each member of your LTRP group should choose a different keyword to research.

My keyword to research: _____

Now begin your research for *one* good reference. You may use encyclopedias, books, or Internet sites. Record the reference you use in the bibliography format given on page 47. Read the information and write notes on what you learn.

National Science Teachers Association

5. Start your bibliography. For each source, write down the author's last name and first initial, year published, title, publisher's city, state, and name. Include the call number so you can easily find the book again. For a webpage, include the electronic address (URL) so you can find the site again. Here are (fictional) examples of bibliography entries:

Dee, Chick A. 1999. *Backyard Birds*. Seattle, WA: Animal Authors, Inc. 590.7 DE

Columbia River Salmon Runs. University of Washington. 15 February 1999. <http://www.fish.washington.edu/salmon/data/>

SOURCE I AM READING:

_____

_____

_____

NOTES FROM THE SOURCE I FOUND:

Day 10

LTRP:
INTRODUCTION
PARAGRAPH

Overview

At this point, student research groups begin producing paragraphs that will be used in the final poster presentation of the project. Working together, groups will produce one paragraph that provides background information on the research topic and introduces the research question. Students can use information from the Local Landscape lesson (Day 6) and Library Research I (Day 9) to compose the paragraph. Once the paragraph is written, it must be typed into the computer and saved on the group disk. An assessment rubric is presented at the end of the lesson for those who wish to use this as a formative assessment.

Focus Question

How do you write an introduction paragraph?

Science Skills

- Students should be able to place their research topic and question in context with background information.

- Students should be able to work as a group to write one introduction paragraph for their project.

- Students should be able to type the paragraph into the computer and save it on their research disk.

Background

For background information on the concepts in this lesson, see "Four Parts of a Scientific Report" (page 2) and "Classroom Organization" (page xiv).

Materials

- access to computer lab

- 1 computer disk for each LTRP group

- Introduction Paragraph Worksheet (provided)

48

Development of Lesson

1. Discuss with students what the final product for this project will look like (the posters). (For examples of actual student posters, see pages 200–201.) What information will they want to include on the posters? If they don't come up with "introduction" on their own, suggest it.

2. Discuss what type of information needs to be included in an introduction paragraph. (It is an introduction to the research project, not an introduction of the students themselves.) Students will be able to suggest various information about the topic and their research questions.

3. Discuss with students how they can work together as a group to write one paragraph. They may want to start on a piece of scratch paper where it is easy to cross things out. Eventually, everyone should have a copy of the paragraph in their notebooks.

4. Students will work in groups to compose the paragraph and then type it into the computer. Give each group a floppy disk. Have them label it with the names of all group members. It's helpful if there is one central location to keep all of the floppies in the classroom so they don't get lost. Review with students some of the basics of computer file management. Documents need to be saved using names that describe the document. Names must be unique so that future files don't overwrite previously created files. For example, students can save the introduction paragraph under the name "introduction." If they name their introduction paragraph file "science" or "paragraph," they may have a hard time finding the introduction later in the project.

Discussion Questions

1. What types of information will you include in your final poster?

2. What kinds of background information will help people who read your poster better understand your research?

3. What different organizational strategies can a group use when writing together?

4. How can you avoid having your computer information lost, erased, or damaged?

5. Now that you have written your introduction paragraph, what additional information could you get from the library?

6. How is the research process a creative process as well as a thinking process?

Introduction Paragraph Worksheet

At the end of this project, you and your group will make a poster that shows and tells about your research project. This is one way a research scientist lets other scientists know about his or her research results. The first part of the poster is an introduction of your research topic and question. Follow the directions to write one introduction paragraph for the group project. Put a copy in your three-ring notebook.

1. Use the information you learned on Day 6, Local Landscape, and the information you acquired in the library to describe your project and why it is interesting to you. Remember to include as many details as possible in the introduction so someone who is not familiar with this kind of research can understand the project. The last sentences must give your research question, hypothesis, and null hypothesis. On the next page are three examples of research project introductions written by other students.

1st sentence:	General statement about your topic.
2nd-5th sentences:	Background information about your topic that relates to your research question.
Last sentence:	Your "do," "is," or "are" research question.

INTRODUCTION

_____

_____

_____

_____

_____

_____

_____

_____

_____

2. Choose one member of your group to type the introduction into the computer. Save the file on your group's research disk as INTRODUCTION.

Three Examples of Introduction Paragraphs Written by Students

PLANT GROWTH ON NORTH- AND SOUTH-FACING HILLS

The sun affects a lot of things. It can affect the amount of time you stay outside and it can affect the growth of plants as well. If there were a situation where one type of plant life got more sunlight than another, the group with more sunlight is most likely to grow faster and be more abundant. We are unaware of any work done in this area. We think this area of study is fairly unique. The question we are trying to answer is: what is the difference in vegetation on a north- and south-facing slope? Our hypothesis is that there will be a difference in vegetation on north- and south-facing slopes. The null hypothesis states there will be no difference.

—Chad, Allison, James, Willy

AGGRESSION BETWEEN MALLARDS AND COOTS

Urban lakes tend to support a variety of birds because most urban lakes contain large amounts of algae. The algae in these lakes helps keep the bird population up, due to the great quantity of food it supplies. These lakes supply food such as algae, moss, seeds, and other vegetation. It is also common for these lakes to have a number of small fish and other living organisms. Because of the abundance of food sources at these urban lakes, one would not expect to find competition among waterfowl for food supplies. Mallards and coots are commonly seen together on urban lakes in the Pacific Northwest. This study is designed to investigate the habitat use and interactions between mallards and coots on an urban lake and answer the question "Do mallards fight coots more often than they fight other mallards that try to feed near them?" My hypothesis is that there will be a difference in the aggression between mallards and coots. My null hypothesis is there will be no difference and mallards will fight equally with other mallards and with coots.

—Julia

SOIL DIFFERENCES

If you look around at the ground next time you are at a park, you may notice that there are lots of different colors of soil. Some are brown, some are tan, and some are black. Some soils have a lot of rock mixed in and others have lots of sand. Different kinds of plants seem to prefer different soil types. Grasses seem to grow best on very sandy soils and mosses grow in moist soils. In this study, I will examine whether different types of soils hold more water. This could affect the type of plants that grow on the soil. My research question is: Does sand, garden soil, or peat moss absorb the most water?

—Katie and Isaac

ASSESSMENT RUBRIC

LTRP: Introduction Paragraph (Day 10)

	Beginner	Intermediate	Proficient	Advanced
General Statement and Background Information	Not able to write more than a general statement followed by the research question.	Writes general statement and background information that are not directly related to research question.	Writes general statement and background information that directly relate to research question.	Writes general statement and detailed background information that directly relate to research question.
Research Question	Research question not stated clearly.	Research question stated clearly.	Research question stated clearly.	Research question stated clearly.
Sequence of Ideas				Shows logical sequence of ideas.

National Science Teachers Association

EXPERIMENTAL DESIGN

Background Information

Lessons in this second section focus on elements of experimental design. The section begins by spending four days setting up two different experiments (Days 11–14). Running the experiments from start to finish provides students experiential understanding of how experimental design can influence results and the interpretation of data. The experiments allow students to manipulate the experimental design and evaluate outcomes and to use this information for their ongoing Long-Term Research Projects (LTRPs).

In the first two lessons in this section, The Toughest Towel (Days 11, 12) and Wigglin' Worms (Days 13, 14), students conduct in-class experiments from start to finish. Following these experiments, they participate in the The Wheel of Inquiry Game! (Day 15), which reviews and reinforces the basics of asking research questions and experimental design. During the rest of the section, students work in their LTRP groups to design the projects. After writing their methods (Day 16) and obtaining teacher approval, students assemble the materials for their project (Day 17) and construct a data sheet for recording information in the field (Day 18). During the final lessons in this section (Days 19, 20) students collect data for their LTRPs.

Treatment Types

Ecology-based field research questions are observational studies set up to compare two conditions. The two conditions being compared are called treatment types. For example, if you wanted to compare the pH of a stream upstream (near its source) to the pH downstream (near its mouth), the two areas would be the two treatment types. When the experimental design makes a comparison between two natural conditions, these natural conditions are the two treatment types; they may be different locations, different species, different weather conditions, or different points in time.

An experiment can also be set up to observe the effect of an action. Someone wants to know what happens when the action occurs compared to what happens when it doesn't occur. In this case, the two treatments would be action (treatment) and no action (control). The control represents the unaltered or natural conditions and is included in an experiment along with the action treatment to create a frame of reference or point of comparison. Imagine that you wanted to find out if the amount of food consumed by goldfish changes when you decrease the water temperature in a fish tank. You could only detect a change if you could compare the amount of food consumed in colder water to the amount of food consumed at natural or ordinary water temperature.

Why are control treatments so important? If the goldfish in cold water ate 5 mg of food, what would it mean? We need to know how much a goldfish eats under natural conditions so we can understand the effect of cold water. Sometimes the outcome of an experiment seems so obvious that scientists forget to include a control. If you were studying the effects of fertilizer on plant growth, it would be an easy mistake to add fertilizer and measure growth. If the plant grew 10 cm in one week, you might conclude that the fertilizer worked. This would be a big mistake; maybe the plant was going to grow 10 cm anyway or maybe the week of the experiment was particularly sunny. The results of the action treatment must be compared to the results of a control treatment. The difference in outcomes between the two treatments can then be measured.

Controlling for Unwanted Effects

The word *control* can also be used as a verb. We might say, "We studied the effect of rain on stream acidity, controlling for temperature." Controlling for something means that you keep it the same for both treatments. In the stream example, controlling for distance from the bank means that water temperatures were measured at the same distance from the bank at the upstream and downstream sites. In the plant fertilizer example above, you would need to control for amount of sunlight, amount of water, temperature, soil condition, and so forth; all these conditions need to be the same for both treatments so that you can detect the effect of the fertilizer. In the paper towel and worm experiments (Days 11–14), students get a lot of practice controlling for different conditions.

For their LTRP, students will have to think about what they need to control for between treatments. For example, if they are comparing rainfall in an open area versus rainfall under trees, they need to control for size of the rainfall collector. If students are comparing the number of spiders in bushes versus in trees, they need to control for search time, weather, temperature, and search techniques. If they decide to do an experiment where they manipulate the environment—for example, planting seeds, adding fertilizer to soil samples, or testing paper planes—they will need to control for unwanted effects on the action and control treatments.

Replication

Replication is a method for ensuring the accuracy of scientific conclusions. If an experiment is conducted one time, on one individual, it's hard to extrapolate the conclusion to a larger population. Maybe that one time was a fluke. When the same results are achieved over many replicates, you can conclude that the results aren't just describing a fluke or a random event. In observational studies, *replication* means collecting many samples. Finding more precipitation under one tree than in one open area doesn't mean much. If you got the same results for several rain gauges under trees as compared to several rain gauges in open areas, you would be much more certain of your conclusions. When conducting an experiment like the paper towel or worm experiments, replication usually means repeating it several times to make sure you get similar results each time. The observations must be made in the exact same way for each replicate. Replicating your observations or your experiment is a way of safeguarding against fluke results and random errors.

During the field trip (Days 19, 20), students will have ample time to complete their research project with several replicates. Students should plan on at least three replicates of each treatment type. Those with methods that are easier to implement may want to do more.

Repeatable

Experiments and observational studies should also be repeatable. *Repeatable* means that you can replicate the study over and over or that someone else could follow your methods and replicate the study. Repeatability ensures that the experiment or observations can be repeated exactly in another situation, at another time, or by another person. Repeatability also ensures that all replicate observations are collected in the exact same way.

It is essential that students plan their experiment (Day 16) with a detailed methodology. They must know exactly the size of the area they will observe and be able to reproduce this size for each of the comparisons and each of the replicates. If methods are not standardized, then conclusions will not be valid. For example, if a group wants to compare the number of stream invertebrates to the number of lake invertebrates, they must search for invertebrates in exactly the same size area in both places. They cannot reduce the size of the area in the lake because it gets deep and is difficult to survey. Ideally, they must think about this beforehand. Realistically, they will discover some of these difficulties when they are actually doing the experiment. This happens to scientists all the time. It is okay to modify your methods in the field as long as you modify them for all replicates of all treatment types—and as long as you record the changes to your methods. In the example, the group may decide they cannot search a 1 × 1 m area in the lake. Instead, they could search a .5 × 1 m area in the stream and a .5 × 1 m area along the edge of the lake.

Random Selection

Random selection is a method for choosing what you will measure that prevents bias. The formal definition of random is that every possible worm or paper towel or fern has an equal chance of being part of the research project. For example, if you wanted to see whether flowers had more seeds in sunny areas than in shady areas, you would need to devise a method for randomly choosing a few flowers from each area. If you just chose flowers that seemed suitable, you could easily bias the study and make the results worthless. If you chose big, healthy flowers in sunny areas (because that's where you expect to find the most seeds) and scrawny flowers in shady areas, you would find a difference in the number of seeds between the two groups of flowers. But that finding might not have anything to do with shade or sun. The difference could simply be due to the bias you had when you selected the flowers.

There are several simple methods for randomly selecting what to measure. In the field, students can work in pairs. One student spins around slowly while the other student, with closed eyes, says, "Stop." The direction in which the spinning student is pointing when he or she hears "stop" has been selected randomly. Students can walk in that direction until they come to the first flower or fern or tree. A second hand on a wristwatch can also be used to pick a random direction if someone who is not looking at the watch says, "Stop." If there are a limited number of items—for example, only 10 trees in the playground—students can choose three for their study by numbering each tree and then randomly picking three numbers from a hat. If students are conducting an experiment in which they manipulate the environment, it is a good idea to choose the action treatment and the control treatment randomly. For example, the plants to be fertilized versus not fertilized should be selected randomly. Random assignment can be done by writing "action treatment" and "control treatment" on slips of paper and randomly choosing one slip of paper for each pot of seeds, plant, fish tank, or tree.

Record Keeping

Data can be recorded in many formats. Some formats are better than others but most of them will work fine. There are, however, some basic ground rules that must be followed. First, always record data neatly and legibly. Data are useless if they cannot be easily and accurately deciphered later. Second, the data sheet must clearly separate treatment conditions and replicates. Data must be recorded separately for each replicate and each treatment. Third, do not risk losing data sheets. If necessary, the teacher can collect all the data sheets before leaving the field site. Make copies of the data sheets and keep them in a safe place. Students can use the originals and if they are lost later, the teacher still has copies—all is not lost!

The Paper Towel Experiment

The paper towel experiment—The Toughest Towel (Days 11 and 12)—attempts to answer the research question: Which paper towel brand is the strongest? There are many ways to determine paper towel strength. Not all of the ways lend themselves to quantifying observations. If we tried scrubbing a tabletop with different paper towels to compare the strength of different brands, we would have to make a subjective observation about how well each paper towel worked. There might not be a clear winner. To quantify this method, we could count the number of swipes made before the paper towel fell apart. We would have to define "falling apart" before beginning the experiment. Does falling apart mean the first tear, or more than that? We must also assume that the pressure exerted by our hand is the same for each swipe of every paper towel. This method of quantifying paper towel strength would quickly become very difficult. If we tried tearing paper towels or measuring the thickness and assuming that thicker towels are stronger, we would run into similar problems with quantifying the observations and making dubious assumptions.

We can avoid making all these assumptions by adjusting our experimental design. In the paper towel lesson, students discuss the pros and cons of several different measures of paper towel strength. Afterward, the teacher demonstrates how paper towel strength will be quantified for the experiment. Towels are attached to ring stands and weights are placed on top of the towels. Students count the number of weights the towel can hold before it breaks. An important focus of this lesson is controlling for unwanted effects.

Students discover that observations are only comparable if each observation is made the exact same way: towels must be attached to the ring stand with the same number of clips, the same amount of water must be dropped on the towel, and weights must be placed on the towel in the same manner. After students control for all the potential unwanted influences on their experiment, the number of weights a paper towel can support will be an objective and quantitative observation. During the paper towel experiments, students also examine the importance of replicating their observations and making their methods repeatable, concepts they need to understand for their Long-Term Research Projects.

The Worm Experiment

The worm experiment—Wigglin' Worms (Days 13 and 14)—asks the question: Do different environmental conditions affect worm-burrowing activity? This is an interesting question but implies that burrowing activity can be objectively measured. Again, we try to find a method of observing burrowing activity that is quantifiable and is not based on questionable assumptions. Also, it must be realistic. In this case, worms are placed on the top of a container of dirt and left overnight in different conditions. The following day the worms are excavated from the containers. Students measure the distance below the top of the dirt at which the worms are found. This method objectively quantifies the depth a worm has burrowed. It does not take into account any lateral movement or whether the worm has moved up and down within the container. By defining worm movement as the distance below the top after 24 hours, students may miss some aspects of worm movement. Having the students think about assumptions and their implications on the results is an important exercise. It helps students visualize the entire experiment and project how decisions made in designing the experiment might affect the results and the interpretation of the results. Students can brainstorm modifications to the experiment such as using narrow containers that limit lateral worm movements to compensate for this assumption. The worm experiment reviews the skills of making quantitative observations, asking research questions, treatment types, controlling for unwanted effects, replicating observations, and making observations repeatable.

The worm burrowing experiment is scripted to ensure that all groups follow the same methods. This allows the class to combine or pool data. Sharing class results emphasizes the range of results and variation in worm behavior. Students should be encouraged to compare their individual results to the overall class results. Are the patterns the same or different? Why? The worm data foreshadow the statistical lessons in Section III: Summarizing and Analyzing Results that will follow data collection: the results of the worm experiment can be displayed in a table or graph; averages can be calculated; and statistical tests can be performed to compare the results of different treatments.

Days 11, 12
THE TOUGHEST TOWEL

Overview

This two-day experiment introduces students to the difficulties of designing a good experiment. Many students will have performed the experiment in earlier grades. It is worthwhile doing it again to remind them of the importance of controlling for unwanted effects in their Long-Term Research Projects. In the first step, students brainstorm techniques for measuring paper towel strength (wet versus dry, tearing versus holding weight). After agreeing on a technique that produces quantitative observations, students design an experiment to measure the amount of weight that a wet paper towel can hold. Students write their own methodology, conduct the experiment, and evaluate the strengths and weaknesses of their methods. Students consider the issues in combining data from different groups. On the second day, students design new experiments to answer some of the questions that arise from the first day.

Focus Question:

What must scientists think about when designing an experiment?

Science Skills

- Students should be able to write detailed methods for an experiment.

- Students should be able to explain how different methods affect results and data interpretation.

- Students should be able to draw conclusions from data.

Background

For background information describing the concepts in this lesson, see "Qualitative and Quantitative Observations," page 1; "The Paper Towel Experiment," page 56; "Controlling for Unwanted Effects," page 54; "Repeatable," page 55; and "Replication," page 54.

Materials

- overhead transparency of picture of ring stand setup (page 65)

- 1 ring stand per student group

- 3 or 4 binder clips per group

- water

- paper towels—3–5 different brands. The results are much easier to keep track of if brands have dramatically different color patterns.

- standardized weights—for example, large heavy washers. All weights should be the same and should have no sharp edges. You will need enough weights so that each group can have enough to break through a wet paper towel. (This may need to be tested beforehand.) We recommend 5/8" zinc, cut washers, available at hardware and building supply stores.

- 1 large box or shallow plastic bucket per group (optional)

- The Toughest Towel Worksheet, Day 1 (provided)

- The Toughest Towel Worksheet, Day 2 (provided)

Development of Lesson

1. Students meet as a class and brainstorm different methods for testing paper towel strength. Students should debate which methods would lend themselves to quantitative observations. Show the weights and the ring stands to the class, stating that this is the available equipment. Ask the students how the equipment could be used to make quantitative observations. The picture on page 65 can be copied onto an overhead transparency to show the students.

2. Introduce the idea of controlling for unwanted effects. Ask the students for some examples of things that might need to be controlled in different experiments. Introduce the students to the idea of a fair test. If students test one brand of paper towel when it is wet, they must also test another brand with the same amount of water for it to be a fair test. For example, what would you need to control for in a study comparing growth between two insect species? *Available food, temperature, water.* What would you need to control for in a study comparing moss growth on deciduous versus coniferous trees? *Rain or moisture, location of trees, age of trees.*

3. Discuss the factors students need to control for in the paper towel study. How wet will the towel be (number of teaspoons of water applied)? Will students drop or place the weights? How many clips will they use? Will it matter if all the groups have the exact same methods?

4. Break the students into small groups (three to four students per group) and have them write up a group methodology on The Toughest Towel Worksheet, Day 1. They should specify exactly how they will conduct the experiment and what they will control for.

5. Pass out the equipment and let the students begin. Paper towels of several different brands should be at the front of the room. (Make sure that paper towels are labeled even when the wrapper is removed. You could write the brand name inside each tube and/or post and label one demonstration towel of each brand.) This is a very loud experiment. As paper towels break, the weights fall to the desk or to the floor. It may be easier for the students to work directly on the floor. A box or plastic bucket can be placed under the ring stand so that the weights don't fall all over when the towel breaks.

6. Students should record results as they go. They should finish one replicate for each paper towel brand on the first day.

7. On Day 2, have the students meet as a class and discuss what happened on the first day. First, of course, you will discuss which brand of paper towel is strongest. Tell the students that you want to combine the data from all the groups to make a decision about which brand is best; students can record their data on a class table or graph at the front of the room. Ask students why there is so much variability in the results. Students will probably be frustrated that other groups didn't do the experiment the same way and so they can't compare results easily. They will probably find that the amount of water used and the method for stacking the weights makes a big difference in the results. Ask the students for suggestions to improve the class data. Introduce the concept of repeatability. Data can only be compared if they are collected in the exact same way.

8. Tell the students that they will have today to answer some of the unanswered questions. Let the students break into their small groups and choose a research question (use the Toughest Towel Worksheet, Day 2). You may want go over the suggestions below as a group or you may want to let the students think up their own questions if they can. All the groups can study different things or the class could decide to redo the entire experiment using a standardized amount of water and weight-stacking method. There are lots of other things to test. The following is a brief list of ideas:

   ■ If you measure the same brand three or four times, will you always get the same results? In other words, is there a lot of variability between towels of the same brand? Would you care about this when purchasing a brand of towel? Why? Is there more variability for some brands than other brands?

   ■ How much difference does the stacking method really make? Try the experiment a few times, controlling for everything but the stacking method (one brand, a standard number of clips, and a standard amount of water but add the weights as a stack or as a pile). Students will need at least two replicates for each stacking method.

   ■ How much difference does the amount of water make? Try the experiment again, controlling for everything but the amount of water. Students could do two or three replicates of wet and dry, or you could try 1, 2, 3, 4, 5 teaspoons of water.

   ■ How much difference does the number of clips make?

   ■ How do the school bathroom towels stack up?

   ■ What if you drop the weights from a fixed height?

9. Have each group write up detailed methods on their Worksheets.

10. After the teacher has checked the methods to make sure that all the details are specified and that there will be some replication, students can carry out their experiments.

11. Meet again as a class and have students share the results of their experiments. Discuss what you learned as a class about the effects of stacking methods, wetness, or variability. Ask students whether they think that the experimental design really mattered. What were the most important things to control for?

Discussion Questions

1. When you wrote your methods, were you able to think of every last important detail? Do you think scientists usually forget things? What do they do when they forget something?

2. What is the effect of variability on research results? If the paper towels were exactly the same and you did exactly the same thing each time, would you get exactly the same results? Why or why not?

3. Was replication necessary? Why or why not?

4. What is the effect of controlling for things like water and stacking methodology?

5. What did you learn from observing the effects of different methods on the results?

6. If you wanted to measure paper towel strength differently, how would you have to change the experiment?

7. Do you think advertising biased your results? How might it have had an effect?

The Toughest Towel Worksheet, Day 1

Research Question: Which brand of paper towel is the strongest?

Hypothesis: Different brands of paper towels are different strengths.

Null Hypothesis: All paper towel brands are the same strength.

Write down the methods that you will use to test for paper towel strength. Try to include every last detail that you think will be important. You can write the methods as a list of steps. (You may not need all seven steps.)

Step 1: _____
_____
_____

Step 2: _____
_____
_____

Step 3: _____
_____
_____

Step 4: _____
_____
_____

Step 5: _____
_____
_____

Step 6: _____
_____
_____

Step 7: _____
_____

Record the results of your experiment in the following table. List the brands you plan to test along the top row and your data (the number of weights needed to break the towel) in the middle row (Trial 1). If you have time, you can try the experiment for a second time with all or some brands.

NUMBER OF WEIGHTS SUPPORTED BY DIFFERENT PAPER TOWELS

Paper Towel Brand				
Trial 1				
Trial 2				

Notes: Record anything you think is interesting or important about these experiments (qualitative observations).

_____
_____
_____
_____
_____
_____
_____
_____

Name _____ Page # _____

The Toughest Towel Worksheet, Day 2

What research question are you trying to answer with your new experiment?

_____

_____

Describe your new methods very carefully!

_____

_____

_____

_____

_____

_____

Record your results in the following table. You should label it the way you think best. You may not need all the rows or all the columns.

What conclusions do you make from your experiment?

_____

_____

_____

_____

_____

National Science Teachers Association

PAPER TOWEL EXPERIMENT

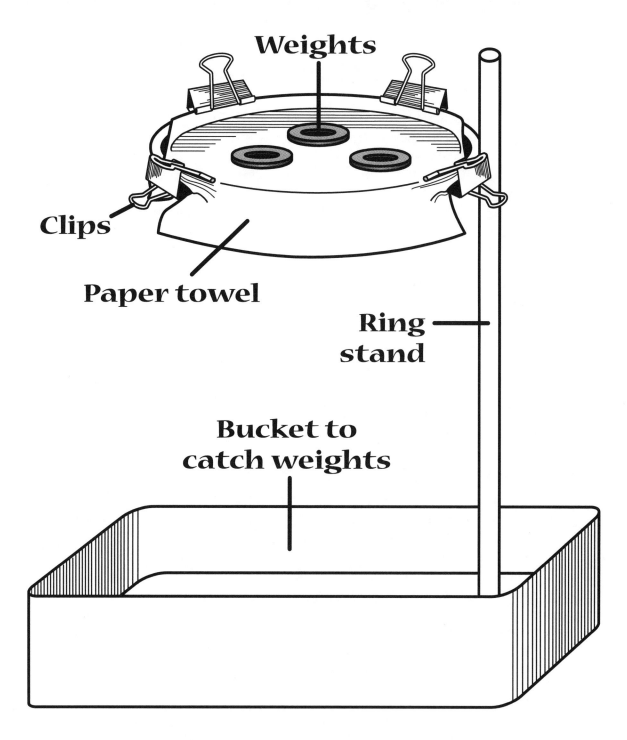

Weights

Clips

Paper towel

Ring stand

Bucket to catch weights

Days 13, 14

WIGGLIN' WORMS

Overview

In this two-day lesson, students practice conducting an experiment from start to finish and compare small group results to class results. The methods are written for the students to follow; however, students still need to control for unwanted effects. This experiment is a good reference lesson for the concepts in experimental design that can be applied to their Long-Term Research Projects. The data from this experiment can be used to demonstrate statistical analysis and scientific presentations in later lessons (Appendixes B, C). Teachers may choose to use this lesson as an embedded formative assessment as it applies and reinforces all of the science research principles learned so far.

Focus Question

What are the details of a good experimental design?

Science Skills

■ Students should be able to follow prescribed methods for a scientific experiment.

■ Students should be able to anticipate and control for unwanted effects.

■ Students should be able to make and record quantitative observations.

■ Students should be able to draw conclusions from data.

Background

For background information describing the concepts in this lesson, see "Lessons That Require Advance Planning," page xv; "Qualitative and Quantitative Observations," page 1; "Information Questions versus Research Questions," page 3; "Hypothesis versus Null Hypothesis," page 4; "Treatment Types," page 53; "Controlling for Unwanted Effects," page 54; "Replication," page 54; "Repeatable," page 55; "Record Keeping," page 56; and "The Worm Experiment," page 57.

Materials

■ 2 identical containers per student group of (large yogurt containers or 2 L soda bottles with the tops cut off work well)

■ 6 worms per student group

■ dirt (enough to fill all the containers at least 3/4 full)

- extra buckets or other containers to put "used" dirt in (1 per group)
- masking tape
- water
- metric rulers
- large spoons
- newspapers
- a few lights
- portable heater or other heat source
- Worm Experiment Worksheet (provided)

Development of Lesson

1. Most details are spelled out very carefully in the Worm Experiment Worksheet, but students will need an overview before they begin. As a class, introduce the question "How do different environmental conditions affect worm behavior?" Have the students suggest different conditions that might make worms burrow deeper or that might inhibit burrowing.

2. Describe the general framework of the experiment. Ask students what things they will need to control for. Ideas include size of the container, amount of water, amount of dirt, type of dirt, size of the worms, and bumping and jostling. You should also bring up confounding factors. What if the light treatment is under a hot lamp? Would it be a light or a heat treatment?

3. Describe the three choices for the experiment: hot versus cold, wet versus dry, and light versus dark. If any of these conditions is hard to set up, you can also test the effects of different soil types: sandy soil versus garden soil. Ask students (or assign students) to get in small groups, about three to four students per group, and to choose one experiment. Encourage the students to select their experiments so that there will be at least two groups conducting each experiment.

4. Students should be able to follow the Worm Experiment Worksheet independently, but it may help to read through all the instructions as a class before beginning the experiment.

5. On the second day, students finish their experiments. Depth of worms should be measured as depth from the top of the soil down to the worm. Each student should record the data from the small group on his or her Worksheet.

6. As each group finishes, have them record their group results on a master chart at the front of the room (butcher paper, blackboard, or overhead projector). Each student should copy down the results from all the groups.

7. After clean-up, meet as a class and discuss the results of the experiments. How important was it to control for different factors? What can you conclude about worm behavior from the results? Would it have been better to have more worms? More group

data? What kinds of worm behavior did you not measure with this technique? *Lateral movements or worms that went down and back up.* How might that have biased your results? This lesson will require a good deal of discussion time.

Discussion Questions

1. What things were hard to control for and what things were easy?

2. What would you do differently if you were to repeat the experiment?

3. What conclusions did each group reach independently?

4. Do the class results confirm the group conclusions? Why might each group get different results?

5. If the groups did the experiment exactly the same way, would they get exactly the same results every time? *No, there is some random chance involved. Some worms might be more active than others or might just happen to burrow a little deeper. Or there may be other differences between worms that we aren't aware of.*

6. Why did you need three worms in each container? *Only one worm wouldn't be enough replication. If there were hundreds of groups collecting the data, each might only need one worm.*

7. When you measure how deep the worm is after 24 hours, is that a good measure of total worm movement? Could you get different results if you had a camera and could see exactly how much the worms moved over the 24 hours? What kinds of movement would you catch with a camera that you didn't catch with the spoon system?

8. How might your results change if you left the worms out for only 1 hour? 48 hours?

Name _____ Page # _____

Worm Experiment Worksheet

Research Question: Do worms burrow deeper in _____ or _____ environments?

Hypothesis:

_____

_____

_____

Null Hypothesis:

_____

_____

_____

METHODS (DAY 1):

1. Mark your names on two pieces of tape and label the sides of the containers. Label one container wet (or hot or light) and the other container dry (or cold or dark) according to your choice of experiment.

2. Fill the container full of dirt. Each container should have an identical level of dirt.

3. Make a "tape ruler" by marking 1 cm intervals on a piece of tape and putting the tape on the container vertically so that 0 cm is at the top of the dirt.

4. Add 2 spoonfuls of water to each container so the worms don't dry out.

5. If you chose wet/dry, add 2 *more* cups of water to the container labeled "wet."

6. Put three earthworms on top of the dirt in each container.

7. Place the containers in the appropriate treatment locations:

■ wet and dry can be on a shelf

■ cold should go outside, in a basement, or in a refrigerator and warm can stay in the classroom or near a heater

■ light should go under a lamp and dark should go under a box or in a dark closet.

8. Make sure that the containers won't be in the way during the rest of class or the next day. You may want to make a "Please Do Not Disturb" sign for the experiment. Let the containers sit for 23 hours.

METHODS (DAY 2):

1. Using a spoon, carefully remove a layer of dirt 1 cm deep and place it in the empty container. Check the removed dirt for worms.

2. Remove the next centimeter of dirt and check for worms. Repeat.

3. Each time you find a worm, record the depth in Table 1. The depth is the number of centimeters of dirt you removed (including the current layer). Depth should be measured from the top down!

TABLE 1: SMALL GROUP RESULTS

Treatment		
Worm 1		
Worm 2		
Worm 3		

What do you conclude about worm behavior? Do you think your hypothesis or your null hypothesis is correct?

_____

_____

_____

4. Record the results from the entire class in Table 2.

TABLE 2: CLASS RESULTS

Wet	Dry	Hot	Cold	Light	Dark

70

ASSESSMENT RUBRIC
Wigglin' Worms (Days 13, 14)

	Beginner	Intermediate	Proficient	Advanced
Following Directions	Has difficulty following directions to set up experiment.	Follows most of the directions to set up experiment.	Follows all directions to set up experiment.	Follows all directions to set up experiment.
Controlling for Unwanted Effects	Not able to control for unwanted effects.	Identifies at least one way to control for unwanted effects, such as the amount of water added to dirt.	Identifies ways to control for unwanted effects, such as the amount of water added to dirt.	Identifies ways to control for unwanted effects, such as the amount of water added to dirt, or light and temperature interaction.
Setting Up Experiment	Not able to set up experiment within given time.	Just barely sets up experiment within allotted time.	Is able to set up experiment within given time.	Finishes setting up experiment easily before time is up.
Collecting Quantitative Data	Does not correctly collect quantitative data.	Correctly collects quantitative data after further explanation.	Correctly collects quantitative data.	Correctly collects quantitative data.
Noticing Patterns and Drawing Conclusions	Able to notice some patterns. Has difficulty drawing conclusions.	Able to notice patterns but has difficulty drawing conclusions.	Able to notice patterns and draw conclusions from data.	Able to notice patterns, draw conclusions from data, and suggest reasons for results.

THE WHEEL OF INQUIRY GAME!

Overview

Students play a game to review the concepts learned to date (quantitative and qualitative observations, parts of a scientific report or presentation, research questions and hypotheses, treatment types, controlling for unwanted effects, replication, random selection). The game is modeled after the game show "Wheel of Fortune."

Focus Question

N/A

Science Skills

■ Students should be able to correctly answer questions that review the concepts of quantitative and qualitative observations, the four parts of a scientific report or presentation, research questions and hypotheses, treatment types, controlling for unwanted effects, replication, and randomization.

■ Students should be able to apply the concepts to new situations.

Background

For background information describing the concepts in this lesson, see "Research Questions and Hypotheses," pages 1–4, and "Experimental Design," pages 53–57.

Materials

■ 2 dice

■ chalkboard or overhead to display the secret phrase, used letters, vowels, and score

■ prizes (optional)

Development of Lesson

1. Before class, choose several secret phrases for the students to guess. These should be fun, creative, and familiar to everyone in the class. You may want to choose one about a recent or upcoming event in the school community or something related to the science research projects. A nonsense phrase, line from a poem, or a famous quotation work well—for example, "Seattle Supersonics," "We're off to see the wizard," "French fries fried by friendly frogs," "Albert Einstein." Write the phrases you

will use on note cards in block letters. This makes it easier to avoid mistakes when the students are guessing letters.

2. Review with students each of the following concepts. Ask for definitions as well as examples.

- *qualitative observations*—observations that describe without counting or measuring

- *quantitative observations*—observations that describe by counting or measuring

- *four parts of a scientific report or presentation*—introduction, methods, results, and discussion

- *information question*—usually a why or how question that is searching for information without comparing anything; it would be difficult to plan an experiment to answer an information question

- *research question*—usually involves some type of comparison; frequently begins with "is," "are," or "do." Is stated in a way to easily set up an experiment to answer the question.

- *hypothesis*—states that there is a difference between two things being compared

- *null hypothesis*—states that there will be no difference between two things being compared

- *treatment types*—two or more conditions that are compared in a research experiment; sometimes referred to as control and treatment

- *controlling for unwanted effects*—keeping factors that might influence results the same for all treatment types

- *replication*—repeating an experiment so that many samples or observations are collected and analyzed

- *random selection*—a method for choosing where samples will be collected so that every possible collection point has an equal chance of being selected

3. Divide the students into teams. Teams of five to seven students work well.

4. Each team rolls the dice to determine who goes first. Highest number wins. Turns move in a clockwise direction.

5. On the board or the overhead, draw lines for each letter in the surprise phrase. Leave an obvious space between words. Draw a box where you will write the letters that have been guessed but are not in the surprise phrase (referred to below as the used-letter box).

6. On each turn, a team rolls the dice to determine the number of points they receive for a right answer. (This replaces spinning a big wheel.)

7. Ask the team one question (questions included below) and give them 10 seconds to come up with an answer. If the answer is correct, they receive the number on the dice as points. Teams can either pick a category (see below: Animals, School, Forests, Invertebrates, Food, At Home, Public Places) or take whatever question the teacher

wants to read. A correct answer earns a team the chance to guess a letter or buy a vowel. Vowels cost five points, which are deducted once regardless of how many vowels are in the phrase. Teams get no additional points for vowels found in the phrase. If they choose to guess a consonant, they get the same number of points that are on the dice for each consonant that appears in the surprise phrase. Write the letter or vowel in the appropriate blanks or in the used-letter box.

8. If the team correctly answers the question *and* correctly guesses a letter, they may try to guess the phrase. Warn them that they must know the entire phrase to solve the puzzle. If they give away some of the words, they end up helping out the other teams.

9. Continue playing until one team correctly guesses the secret phrase. This game can be played over and over again. You can add new questions if you use up the attached questions and want to play again.

SUGGESTED GAME QUESTIONS AND ANSWERS
Animals

1. Zebras have black and white stripes. Is this a qualitative or quantitative observation? *Qualitative.*

2. Salmon can jump 3 m. Is this a qualitative or quantitative observation? *Quantitative.*

3. Ask a research question that compares grizzly bears and black bears. *Do grizzly bears eat more than black bears? Do grizzly bears attack more people than black bears? Do grizzly bears eat more meat than black bears? Are male grizzly bears larger than male black bears?*

4. In which section of a scientific report can you find the research question? *Introduction.*

5. Why do worms burrow? Is this a research question or an information question? *Information question.*

6. You notice that anole lizards are sometimes brown and sometimes green. You decide to figure out whether lizard color changes with the temperature of the environment. What research question could you ask? *Is there a difference in anole lizard skin color at cold and at hot temperatures?*

7. State the null hypothesis for the following hypothesis: Box turtles and painted turtles run at different speeds. *Box and painted turtles run at the same speed. There is no difference between the speed of box and painted turtles.*

8. Name two things that might be found in the results section of a scientific report. *A graph, a table, a description of the graph or table, the results of statistical analyses.*

School

1. There are five swings in the playground. Is this a qualitative or quantitative observation? *Quantitative.*

2. State a qualitative observation about your school. *The teachers are nice. The school has covered and uncovered play areas. The library has good books. The parents help in the classroom and on field trips.*

3. Is the following question a research question or an information question: Who are the teachers at this school? *Information question.*

4. State the hypothesis for the following research question: Do sixth graders or eighth graders participate more in school fund-raising activities? *There is a difference in the number of fund-raising activities organized by sixth and eighth graders.*

5. Is the following statement a hypothesis or a null hypothesis: Eighth and sixth graders raised the same amount of walkathon money. *Null hypothesis.*

6. In which section of a scientific report can you find a list of the materials that were used to do an experiment? *Methods.*

7. Someone told me that on rainy days, more students arrive late to school than on non-rainy days. I didn't believe them so I counted the number of late students on eight different rainy days. Wow, were there a lot of late students. I guess the information was correct. There are more late students on rainy days. What's wrong with how the research was conducted? *No counts of late people on nonrainy days were made. Maybe there are just as many, or even more, late people on nonrainy days.*

8. Why do some kids always complain about bad grades and other kids just don't care? Is this a research question or an information question? *Information.*

9. Kyleeha wanted to find out what time most teachers arrive at school in the morning. She had her mom drive her to school early one day so she could sit in the hall and record the time each teacher arrived. She learned that three teachers arrived before 7:00 a.m., seven teachers arrived between 7:00 and 7:30 a.m., and the rest arrived between 7:30 and 8:00 a.m. From this observation, she concluded that all teachers arrive before 8:00 a.m. Do you believe her conclusion? Why or why not? *She doesn't have enough replicate days. She needs to watch the teachers arrive more than one day.*

10. Pin wanted to find out how many schools in Seattle have recycling bins in their classrooms. He didn't have enough time or money for stamps to contact every school. How could he randomly select a sample of 10 schools to survey? *Pin could write the name of every school on a piece of paper and then draw 10 of them from a bowl or envelope. A second way would be to number each school and then pick 10 numbers out of a hat, from a random number table, or from a random-number-generating program on a calculator or computer.*

Forests

1. Make a qualitative observation about this object (e.g., branch, bag of leaves, pine cone). *The branch is green. The leaves are yellow and brown. The pine cone is very big.*

2. In which section of a scientific presentation can you find a summary of the data? *Results.*

3. One million sockeye salmon have just returned to a 14 km stretch of the Adams River in British Columbia. Is this a qualitative or quantitative observation? *Quantitative.*

4. Do spotted owl eggs and chicks survive more often when their nests are built near the ground or near the treetops? State a hypothesis and null hypothesis for this research

question. *Hypothesis: There is a difference in survival rates of spotted owl eggs and chicks in nests closer to the ground and closer to the tops of the trees. Null Hypothesis: There is no difference in survival rates of spotted owl eggs and chicks in low and high nests.*

5. Vivian noticed that salamanders can be found under rocks and under rotting logs. She wants to do a research project to compare the number of salamanders under rocks and rotting logs. State her research question. *Are salamanders found more often under rotting logs or under rocks?*

6. Mahmoud wanted to find out whether Douglas fir trees grow better in sun or in shade. What is the research question he is asking? *Do Douglas fir trees grow faster in sun or in shade?*

7. Ellice wanted to know whether tadpoles preferred the sunny or shady side of ponds. Her null hypothesis stated that there is no difference in the number of tadpoles on the shady side and on the sunny side of a pond. What are her two treatment types? *Sunny and shady sides of ponds.*

8. Jared went to the woods one day and counted the number of birds he found in trees and bushes along a stream and the number he found at least 50 m from the stream. He found more birds away from the stream. State one factor he needed to control for to have valid results. *He made an equal number of observations in the morning and in the afternoon at both habitats. He observed the same amount of area or time in both habitats.*

9. Vishal wanted to study the relationship of diameter and height of cedar trees growing along a lakeshore and those growing along a river. At both locations, he picked the first five cedar trees he saw. What's wrong with his experimental methods? *He did not randomly select his trees at each location. Because he picked the first five trees he found, he may be biasing his results by picking trees closest to a trail or road. It would be better if he numbered all the trees within a specific area and then randomly chose the numbers from a hat.*

Invertebrates

1. Make a quantitative observation about ladybugs. *One ladybug had six spots on each wing. A ladybug visited five flowers in 30 minutes. Ladybugs can eat 12 aphids in one hour.*

2. Stephanie was preparing a research report comparing how spiders build webs in cold and warm environments. What are the different parts she must include in a report? *Introduction, methods, results, discussion.*

3. What is the null hypothesis that goes with the following hypothesis: "Spider webs are different sizes in environments where there is less food than in environments where there is more food." *Spider webs are the same size in environments with more food and with less food.*

4. Someone gives you two different insects that you have never seen before. One has very long legs and a long abdomen while the other has very short legs and a short abdomen. State a research question that you might test with these insects. *Do insects with long legs run faster than insects with short legs? Is there a difference in the amount of food eaten by long- and short-legged insects? Are short-legged insects better climbers than long-legged insects?*

5. Make a quantitative observation about a spider. *A spider has eight legs.*

6. In which section of a scientific presentation can you find a detailed description of how an experiment was set up and performed? *Methods.*

7. Nicole's null hypothesis for her research project is, "There are the same number of water striders on areas with fast-moving water as on areas of calm water." What is her hypothesis? *There are different numbers of water striders on calm water patches than on fast-moving water.*

8. "Do potato bugs bury deeper in wet soil than in dry soil?" Is this a research question or an information question? *Research question.*

9. Sarah placed one cricket in a box that had a light at one end and was dark at the other end. In her experiment, the cricket moved to the end of the box with a light. Sarah concluded that all crickets prefer lighted areas. What was wrong with her experiment? *Sarah must test more than one cricket before making such a broad conclusion.*

10. Fong Tian wanted to test whether walking sticks would eat more leaves in a dark environment than in a light environment. He put three walking sticks in three boxes in the closet and three walking sticks in three boxes on the windowsill. What are some conditions he will need to control for? *Temperature, moisture.*

11. Rishi wanted to test whether bugs are attracted to different colors. He put a dish each of yellow water, green water, and blue water in his backyard. The next day he found 10 bugs in the yellow water, 6 in the green, and 3 in the blue. He concludes that bugs prefer yellow water. What's wrong with this research? *He only had one dish of each color of water. To test this idea, he should have had several dishes of each color so he could look for patterns.*

12. Franny was studying worms. She wanted to study how worms react to changes in temperature. She had a bucket with about 50 worms in it and needed only 10 for the experiment. She picked out the first 10 worms she could find and put 5 in one tank and 5 in another tank. Then she put one tank in a warm room and one tank in a cold room. What is wrong with how she chose the worms? *It isn't random because she is only observing the effects of temperature on worms that happened to be at the top of the bucket. There might be something unusual about these worms that caused them to stay at the top of the bucket. To be random, she would have to let every worm, big or small, have an equal chance of being in the study.*

Food

1. Make a qualitative and a quantitative observation about an Oreo cookie. *Qualitative: Tastes sweet. Is bad for you. Gets soggy if you leave the bag open. Quantitative: Has two black cookies separated by one layer of white filling. Costs $1.99 per package.*

2. Soon-bok had a theory that packages of Starburst candy always have the same number of reds. She bought two packages and compared the number of reds in each. It was the same (four), so she concluded that all Starburst packages have four reds. What was wrong with her "research"? *Two packages might have had the same number of reds by coincidence. She needed to compare more than just two packages.*

3. In what section of a scientific paper does a scientist interpret what the data mean? *Discussion.*

4. What is the null hypothesis that goes with the following hypothesis: "Brand A nacho chips have a different number of calories per gram than Brand B nacho chips." *Brand A and Brand B have the same number of calories per gram.*

5. "Why do some brands of ice cream melt so much faster than other brands?" Is this a research or an information question? *Information.*

6. "All six loaves of bread were stale." Is this a qualitative or quantitative observation? *Qualitative. "There are six loaves of stale bread" would be quantitative. The observation here was that the objects were stale.*

7. Present a research question that could test for differences between pizzas made by different companies. *Are the "large" pizzas of Company X larger than the "large" pizzas of Company Y? Do company X's pizzas cost more per square inch than company Y's? Does Company X or Company Y put more pepperoni on their pizzas?*

8. State a sentence that might be found in the introduction section of a report on french fries. *French fries are deep-fried potatoes. French fries are a common American snack food. French fries are commonly sold at fast-food restaurants. There are two kinds of French fries—with and without skin. We wanted to see whether people prefer MacDonald's or Burger King's french fries.*

9. Jeremy wondered if different brands of chocolate chips melted at different rates. He made two batches of cookies, each with a different type of chip. One batch at a time, he put the cookies in the oven to cook. He timed how long it took the chips in each cookie to melt. What is one thing he needed to control for? *Was the batter the same? Was the oven the same temperature each time? Was the batter the same temperature before he put it in the oven? Did he put the cookies in the same place in the oven each time? Did he use the same type of cookie sheet?*

10. Grace wanted to see if mold forms on white bread and wheat bread at the same rate. She put six little squares of white bread and six little squares of wheat bread on 12 different plates. She observed them every day to check for mold. What are some of the things she needs to control for? *Temperature, moisture, contamination, amount of light.*

At Home

1. Why do research reports always include a bibliography? Scientists always give credit for work and ideas done by other scientists. Data cannot be interpreted without an understanding of the "bigger picture" and what is already known about a topic.

2. State one quantitative observation about your apartment or house. *There are four people living in my house. There are two doors to go outside. It cost $120,000.*

3. My bedroom is pink. I have one bed in it. The bed has a warm comforter. My window is 4 square feet wide. I have seven stuffed animals on my bed. How many quantitative observations did I just make about my bedroom? *Three.*

4. My father told me that if I plucked the dead flowers off the daisy plants, they would

bloom more. State a testable hypothesis and null hypothesis that goes with this theory. *Hypothesis: Daisy plants whose dead flowers are picked will have different numbers of total blossoms than daisy plants whose dead flowers are not picked. Null Hypothesis: There is no difference in the total number of blossoms on daisy plants with and without the dead flowers picked off.*

5. "Does my father prefer watching the news on Channel 5 or on Channel 7?" Is this a research or an information question? *Research question.*

6. If Marianne wanted to test whether her cat sleeps more often on the windowsill or on the bed, what would her null hypothesis be? *The cat spends the same amount of time sleeping in the bed and on the windowsill.*

7. In which section of a scientific report would the following statement be found: "We found four times as many chairs on the first floors of the houses sampled as compared to the second floor." *Results.*

8. Mariah thought that her mother was nicer to her little sister than to her. One day she recorded every positive thing that her mother said to either one of them and then counted them up. Her mother said 17 positive things to her little sister and only 11 positive things to Mariah. Mariah concluded that her mother was nicer to her little sister. What's wrong with this research? *She should have collected data on more than one day. She should have written down how many total things her mother said to each of them because maybe her mother was just talking more to her sister that day.*

9. I think my dog digs in the garden more right after we plant new flowers. I watched him for 10 afternoons. For 5 of the afternoons, I just observed how many minutes he spent digging. For the other 5 days, I went out and planted flowers in the yard in the morning. Again, I observed how many minutes he spent digging in the afternoon. What are the treatment types in this experiment? *Planting new flowers in the morning and not planting new flowers in the morning.*

Public Places

1. "Why do people like to go to shopping malls?" Is this a research question or an information question? *Information question.*

2. People go the mall at different rates when it is rainy than when it is sunny. Is this a null hypothesis or a hypothesis? Hypothesis.

3. The bus is usually two minutes late. Is this a qualitative or a quantitative observation? *Quantitative.*

4. If Heather wanted to test whether the bathroom stalls in her school bathroom get used equally, what would her null hypothesis be? *All bathroom stalls get used equally.*

5. How could you make a quantitative observation about grocery shopping behavior? *Time spent shopping, number of items purchased, total cost, weight of purchases, average price.*

6. Thomas was doing a project for school to find out what models and years of cars produce the most air pollution. He got permission from the manager at an emission testing station to record, for 200 cars, each car's model, year, and whether or not it

passed the emission test. What was his research question and null hypothesis? *Research question: Do some models and years of cars create more air pollution than others? Null hypothesis: There is no difference in the amount of air pollution produced by different car models manufactured in different years.*

7. State two things that might be found in the methods section of Thomas's research report on car pollution. *Location of emission testing station, list of car models observed, description of how the emission test works, number of days spent at the emission testing station.*

8. In which section of a scientific report would the following statement most likely be found: "We believe that we found more people doing their shopping at malls than through catalogues because they want to be able to see the actual product before purchasing it. Further research using in-depth questionnaires might provide more information about shopping behavior." *Discussion.*

9. If Raj wanted to test whether pushing the crosswalk button really worked, he could set up a study where he timed the length of the red light without pushing the button and the length of the red light if he pushed the button right after the light turned red. What are some of the things he would have to control for? *Push the button at the same time every time, number of cars, time of day.*

10. Travonne wanted to know whether people littered more in parks without trash cans than in parks with trash cans. He found a park with a trash can and he went there for one hour every afternoon for a week and observed how much litter was on the ground. He found another park without a trash can and he went there for one hour every afternoon for a week and observed how much litter was on the ground. At the end of one week, he had noted an average of 3 pounds of litter per day in the park with a trash can and 1 pound of litter in the park without a trash can. He concluded that people litter more in parks with trash cans. State one thing that is wrong with his research? *He only looked at one park with a trash can and one park without a trash can. There could have been something unusual about these parks. He would have been better off to go to several parks with and several parks without trash cans. Furthermore, he didn't control for how many people were at the park. Maybe the park with the trash can had five times more visitors every day than the park without.*

LTRP: Methods and Materials

Days 16, 17

Overview

Planning for the Long-Term Research Project begins in earnest with this lesson and the next one, Data Sheets (Day 18). Today, the students design their experiment for the research question they selected during LTRP: Research Questions and Hypotheses (Day 8). In planning their experiment, students must consider the basic elements of experimental design emphasized in the paper towel and worm experiments. That is, they must distinguish between treatment types, determine what other effects they need to control for, replicate the experiment, and randomly select the replicates. To write up the experimental design, the students make a list of materials they need, including the quantity, and then describe, step-by-step, how to conduct the experiment. This section needs to be typed into the computer and saved on each group's research disk. The final step is getting the materials. Each group will need a bag or box to keep its materials together. An assessment rubric is included with this lesson.

Focus Question

How can we design an experiment to try to answer our research question?

Science Skills

- Students should be able to apply concepts of experimental design (treatment types, controlling for unwanted effects, replication, random selection) to the design of their own research project.

- Students should be able to design an experiment suitable for answering their research question.

- Students should be able to list materials needed to perform the experiment.

- Students should be able to describe methodically how they will conduct the experiment.

Background

For background information describing the concepts in this lesson, see "Four Parts of a Scientific Report," page 2; "Treatment Types," page 53; "Controlling for Unwanted Effects," page 54; "Replication," page 54; "Repeatable," page 55; "Random Selection," page 55.

Materials

- access to computer lab
- map of field site
- box or bag for each student group to keep its materials together
- LTRP: Methods and Materials Worksheet (provided)

Development of Lesson

1. Review with students the following concepts of experimental design:

   - treatment types
   - controlling for unwanted effects
   - replication
   - repeatable experiments

2. Ask the students how arbitrary choices might influence or bias data. For example, if you are comparing the number of different types of plants that grow on the forest floor near a stream and far away from the stream, you could bias your results by always choosing sites next to the trail for your far-from-stream replicates. How might the trail influence your results? *People walking on the edge of the trail could kill smaller plants. Dogs that urinate along the trail could affect what grows there.* You might decide that all replicates must be at least 5 m from the trail. Then where do you put your replicates?

   The following three scenarios can be used as discussion tools to develop the concept of what is random. As students prepare their methods for their LTRP, they should think about how they will select exactly what to measure. Wherever possible, the selection process should be random.

   A. Dray wanted to study ferns. He wanted to know if they grew better in the sun or in the shade. He thought that they would grow better in the shade. He found 20 ferns that were growing in the shade at his study site. He picked the 5 healthiest looking ferns. Then he found 13 ferns growing in the sun and he picked the 5 weakest looking ferns. He compared their growth rates over the four years and concluded that ferns do like the shade better.

      This isn't random because all ferns did not have an equal chance of being in the study. He biased his results by selecting observations that already fit his hypothesis. The results from this study wouldn't give you any good information. A better way to select ferns would be to number them all and draw a number from a hat or to spin in a circle until someone with his or her eyes closed says, "Stop." Then walk in that direction until the person says "Stop" again and then take the closest fern. You could also pick a random direction and a random distance using a watch with a second hand (for direction) and the seconds on a digital watch (for distance). Just have someone who can't see the watches say "Stop" and take the readings.

   B. Franny loved blackberries. She wanted to know if blackberry plants produced more berries in wet soil or in dry soil. She surveyed her neighborhood and found

10 plants living in wet soil and 17 living in dry soil. She numbered each plant. She asked her friend to pick four numbers between 1 and 10. Then she included the blackberry plants in wet soil with those numbers in her research project. Next she asked another friend to pick four numbers between 1 and 17. She studied the blackberry plants in dry soil with those numbers. She counted how many berries were on each plant. In the end, she found an average of 45.3 berries on the plants in wet soil and 23.9 berries on plants in dry soil. She concluded that blackberry plants produce more berries in wet soil than in dry soil.

This was a good random selection of observations or study units. It would be easy to believe the conclusions from this study.

C. Seth wanted to see if soil pH was the same around the parking lot and in the middle of the playground at his school. He collected five soil samples from both places. To select each of his soil sample locations, he cut eight pieces of paper the same size and labeled them N, NE, E, SE, S, SW, W, NW. He stood in the middle of the parking lot and drew one piece of paper. Then, using a compass, he walked in that direction until he reached the edge of the parking lot. He took his sample exactly 1 m from the asphalt at this location. He repeated this method four more times until he had all his parking lot samples. For the playground samples he followed the same method by drawing a piece of paper to indicate the direction and then walked 15 paces in that direction. He collected his soil sample at this location. He repeated this method four more times as well.

This was a good random selection of sample sites. Seth has not biased his results by how he collected his soil samples.

3. Ask for an example of a research question. Brainstorm possible experiments that could be done to try to answer the research question. Use the terms reviewed above to push the students to be more specific about the experimental design. Why are some approaches better than others? Is there such a thing as a wrong approach? You may need to go through this with more than one research question depending on whether the students are suggesting appropriate designs. You can choose a question from the group(s) most likely to have difficulty designing an experiment.

4. Hand out the LTRP: Methods Worksheets and maps of the field site. Review directions, then let the groups get started. You will have to circulate to answer questions and troubleshoot the experimental design. Elaborate experiments may be too difficult to realize unless the group is highly motivated and works well together.

5. Groups can divide responsibilities for typing and getting materials together. Many groups may need tape measures. If the tape measure will be used to measure transects or quadrats, a string or lightweight rope can be used as well. Meter divisions can be marked with a permanent marker or by tying a knot at the appropriate place. This will save on the number of tape measures needed.

Discussion Questions

1. Why must some factors be controlled for?

2. Give an example of an experiment where some factor was not controlled for and how that fact may have affected the results.

3. Why are some approaches scientifically better than others? Is there such a thing as a wrong approach?

4. How is a randomly chosen replicate different from an arbitrarily chosen replicate?

5. Describe different ways to randomly choose a field plot.

6. What happens if, after carefully planning your experiment, you arrive at the field site and can't go to the area you planned on using?

LTRP: Methods and Materials Worksheet

1. When scientists do research projects, they write detailed instructions for how they will do the project before they start. That is what your group will do today. First, write your research question here:

_____

_____

_____

2. List the materials you will need. This should look like the list of ingredients in a recipe.

quantity   **item**

_____   _____

_____   _____

_____   _____

_____   _____

_____   _____

3. Designing your experiment: Talk with your group about how you will try to answer your research question. Think about the field techniques you practiced a couple of weeks ago. Write the steps for your research below. As you write this, you may need to go back to #2, the list of materials, and make changes.

_____

_____

_____

_____

_____

_____

_____

_____

_____

_____

_____

4.   How many replicates do you need (or think you can do)? Remember, this means how many times will you repeat your experiment to make sure you don't get fooled by an oddball result.

Replicates (number of times we will repeat the sampling) _____.

5.   Your replicates must be done at randomly chosen locations. Describe how you can randomly select where your replicates will be.

_____

_____

_____

_____

_____

6.   What conditions may vary from one replicate to the next that you can control for?

_____

_____

_____

7.   Where will you do your research? Look at the map of your research site and mark the general area where you think you need to work.

8.   Type the list of materials and procedures (#2 and #3) on the computer. Then save the file on your project disk under the name "Methods."

9.   Get your materials together.

Teacher's Approval _____

Congratulations! You've finished your methods!

ASSESSMENT RUBRIC
Methods Paragraph (Days 16, 17)

	Beginner	Intermediate	Proficient	Advanced
Inclusion of Materials	Omits some necessary materials.	Includes almost all materials.	Includes all materials.	Includes all materials and describes them in detail. (10' nylon rope)
Inclusiveness of Methods	Methods skip obvious steps.	Methods skip several steps.	Methods complete so they can be repeated by someone else.	Methods complete so they can be repeated by someone else.
Understanding of Randomization and Controls	Methods do not show an understanding of randomization of sampling areas or controlling for unwanted effects.	Methods show a limited understanding of randomization of sampling areas and controlling for unwanted effects.	Methods show an understanding of randomization of sampling areas and controlling for unwanted effects.	Description of methods shows a thorough understanding of randomization of sampling areas and controlling for unwanted effects.
Alignment of Methods and Research Question	Methods may not be aligned with research question.	Methods aligned with research question.	Methods aligned with research question.	Methods aligned with research question.

The Truth about Science

Overview

This final lesson before the students collect their data (Days 19, 20) asks the students to create a systematic and organized form for recording their data. Constructing the data sheet forces students to think through the experiment one more time before they actually perform it. Data sheets also keep the students focused while working because they have a certain number of sections they have to complete. The data collection form sets the stage for the data analysis in Section III: Summarizing and Analyzing Results. Students may confuse the organization of a data sheet with that of a data table. This lesson focuses on the data sheet. During Tables Tell the Tale (Day 21), students organize their data into a data table.

Focus Question

How can we systematically record data from our experiment?

Science Skills

■ Students should be able to create a systematic and organized form for recording experimental data.

Background

For background information describing the concepts in this lesson, see "Record Keeping," page 56.

Materials

■ overhead transparencies of Sample Data Sheets

■ graph paper with light lines

■ rulers

■ Rite in the Rain paper (optional, available through scientific supply stores and college or university bookstores)

Development of Lesson

1. Ask students to look back at the paper towel and worm experiments. How did they record their data? What was helpful about the data forms on the Worksheets for those experiments?

2. Ask students to state their LTRP research questions and brainstorm how they can record field data in an organized and systematic way. If students have difficulty coming up with ideas, Sample Data Sheets are included at the end of this lesson. They can be copied on the board or on overhead transparencies and left up for students to refer to during the lesson.

   There are many ways to design data sheets. Some ways are better than others. Ask the students to describe some of the pros and cons of the Sample Data Sheets. What qualities do the better data sheet ideas have in common? It is very important to include space for each of the treatment types and each of the replicates. Students should also include space for the names of the group members, date, time, weather, and any other notes they may want to make during their experiment. Data sheets must be legible and comprehensible when completed. Will it be clear to the students where the replicate data are? Where data for each treatment type are recorded?

3. When the students appear to understand the ideas, send them to their LTRP groups to start working. Each group needs a ruler and graph paper. Each group member may make a data sheet and the group can choose one to use. If you will be collecting data outside, you may photocopy the data sheet onto Rite in the Rain paper, just in case, or give students large Ziploc bags to put their data sheets in.

   A Neat Idea: Students can construct their own waterproof data sheets by putting clear contact paper over the data sheets. Then, they can record their data directly on the contact paper using a grease pencil. Be sure the data are copied onto another sheet of paper before the form is erased and used again. Data forms can also be created right on the contact paper. If students make mistakes or changes, they can rub the grease pencil off and start over. Putting a piece of cardboard behind the graph paper will make it stiff and easier to write on in the field.

Discussion Questions

1. How will having a data sheet contribute to the quality of your research results?

2. What qualities make some of the forms better than others?

3. What other information is it a good idea to include on a data sheet?

4. What rules must one follow when filling out a data sheet while working outside? *Write legibly, keep data sheet clean and dry, do not lose data sheet, make sure all members of the group record the same data.*

5. What are some of the advantages and disadvantages of using a data sheet or a lab notebook?

Sample Data Sheets

RESEARCH QUESTION:

Do leaf-damaging insects prefer alder or maple leaves?

Date _____ Group Members_____

Location	Alder Leaves with Damage	Alder Leaves, No Damage	Maple Leaves with Damage	Maple Leaves, No Damage
1				
2				
3				
4				
5				

NOTES:

RESEARCH QUESTION:

Is fern density higher on north- or south-facing slopes?

Date _____ Group Members_____

Replicate	North-facing Slopes (# of ferns in 10 × 10 m area)	South-facing Slopes (# of ferns in 10 × 10 m area)
1		
2		
3		
4		
5		

NOTES:

RESEARCH QUESTION:

Are more invertebrates found in shaded soils or soils open to the sun?

Date _____ Group Members_____

Open Area I	Species	Number of Individuals	Shaded Area I	Species	Number of Individuals
Open Area II	Species	Number of Individuals	Shaded Area II	Species	Number of Individuals

NOTES:

Days 19, 20

LTRP:
FIELD TRIP

Overview

These two lessons are the centerpiece of the curriculum. Before this time, students have been preparing for the data collection. After this time, they will be analyzing and presenting their results. These lessons can be completed as two all-day field trips, as several visits to a nearby park or the school yard, in the classroom conducting experiments, or any combination of events. Allowing at least two days gives students time to practice their methods, leave traps or experiments out overnight, and observe different weather or light conditions. The lesson development is written for classes doing field-based research. For classes doing lab-based experiments, these two days are for the students to set up and run their experiments.

Focus Question

N/A

Science Skills

- Students should be able to carry out a planned, scientific data collection.
- Students should be able to record data accurately in the field.
- Students should be able to work as a group to collect data and make any necessary modifications to the original plan.

Background

For background information describing the concepts in this lesson, see Field Techniques (Day 7); "Controlling for Unwanted Effects," page 54; "Replication," page 54; "Random Selection," page 55.

Materials

- data sheets (constructed on Day 18)
- clipboards and pencils for each student group
- each group will require different materials and will have identified and gathered them on Days 16, 17
- camera with film
- parent volunteers

92

National Science Teachers Association

Development of Lesson

1. Before leaving the classroom, meet as a group. Check to see that all students have the necessary clothes and footgear for fieldwork. Will rain gear be necessary? Does everyone have lunch and/or a snack? A water bottle?

2. Have one person in each group read the list of necessary materials (from the LTRP: Methods and Materials Worksheet [Days 16, 17]) to the rest of the group. Do they have everything that they will need?

3. Remind the students about being consistent and recording any changes to their methods so that they will remember exactly what they did. Each group should bring a copy of the LTRP: Methods and Materials Worksheet from Days 16, 17 to help group members remember their plan when they are in the field.

4. Remind students that they must randomly select their replicates. Ask student groups what they will need to select (e.g., sites? trees?) and how they will do it. Suggest that they take at least one replicate from each treatment on the first day instead of taking all the replicates from one treatment on one day (that way you can control for the weather a little bit).

5. Make sure that any equipment that needs to be left out overnight (insect traps, precipitation gauges, etc.) is well labeled.

6. Explain any safety rules that are necessary for your trip: crossing streets, avoiding dangerous cliffs or fast-moving water, staying within sight of an adult. It is vital to have an adult with each group.

7. Photograph students collecting their data or conducting their experiments. Photographs can be returned to students during LTRP: Poster Preparation (Days 34, 35, 36) to decorate the posters.

8. Have fun collecting the data!! Encourage students to collect as many replicates as possible.

9. When you return from the field trip, have students place their data sheets and any materials in a safe location. Use a fresh data sheet on the second day. Data that are lost cannot be replaced. The information already collected should be left safely in the classroom.

94

ANALYZING AND SUMMARIZING RESULTS

Background Information

In this section, students describe and interpret the data that they collected in the field. Through this process, students gain an understanding of both the statistical and ecological meaning of their own data.

The first three lessons (Days 21–24) teach fundamental skills in organizing and summarizing data. First, students display their data as a well-organized table. Next, they build intuition about averages and calculate averages for their own data. Finally, they graph their data and interpret the graphs in light of what they know about their data. During the next four lessons (Days 25–28), students learn the fundamentals of variability and statistical analysis, which are presented through fun, hands-on activities. A summary of the important mathematical ideas is presented below, together with references for further reading. The final three lessons (Days 29–32) guide the students in reporting their findings and evaluating the meaning of their data. In these lessons, students prepare their results and discussion paragraphs. When these are complete, each student will have a draft of his or her entire scientific report including the introduction, the methods, the results, and the discussion. The computer-printed versions of these paragraphs will be used for their research posters. Assessment rubrics are included at the end of each of the lessons where students write paragraphs (Days 10, 29, 31/32). They are intended to be used immediately after the paragraph is written so students can receive feedback and make adjustments to improve the quality of their work.

Sampling from a Population

Researchers are always trying to answer a question about a whole population—for example, all trees in the park, all trees in general, all birds, or everyone in the school. We can rarely count or measure every single element of the population. It would take

SCiLINKS.
THE WORLD'S A CLICK AWAY

Topic: populations
Go to: *www.sciLINKS.org*
Code: TAS95

too much time and too much money. Instead, we take a random sample of the population as an estimate of the entire population.

When collecting data in the field, it is hard to remember that there is a population out there, a population that you can never see. However, the population is critical to the idea of doing research. No one really cares whether the three samples taken in the stream are different from the three samples taken in the lake. It becomes interesting when samples tell us about the whole stream and the whole lake. All the possible samples that could be taken from the stream are one population. All the possible samples that could be taken from the lake are another population. The point of taking samples is to learn something about the entire population. Statistics is the science of learning about a population from the information in a sample. In the Faux Fish Figuring lesson (Day 25), students sample a population that they can actually touch and explore and they evaluate the information from different-sized samples.

The Normal Distribution

The normal curve is a bell-shaped function that is very useful for describing and analyzing data (Figure 1). The normal curve describes the way many things are distributed in nature. If you were to graph the heights of 100 trees in a forest or the weights of 100 goldfish, you would find a shape that looks something like a bell. Most observations pile up in the center of the graph. A few observations are much smaller or much bigger than the others and these form the tails of the bell-shaped curve.

FIGURE 1: NORMAL CURVE

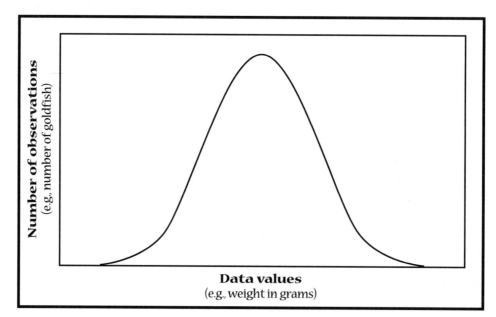

Unless you have thousands of observations, you won't see a smooth curve like Figure 1. When graphing real data (e.g., the Faux Fish) you will end up with a graph that is only roughly bell-shaped (Figure 2).

FIGURE 2: HISTOGRAM (BAR GRAPH) OF FISH WEIGHTS

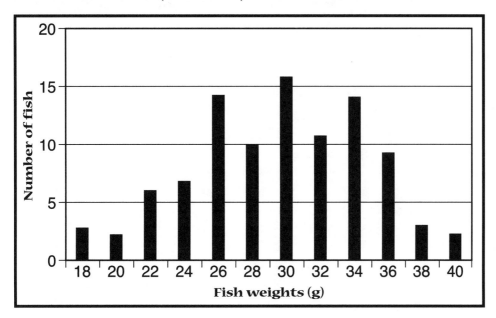

A histogram is a bar graph showing how many observations are in each of several categories. The first step in making a histogram is to decide how many categories you need on the x-axis. Usually, 10 is plenty of categories but the exact number may depend on how the data are structured. For example, if you have 14 possible values, it's probably easiest to have 7 or 14 categories. In the fish weight example, 12 categories were created so that each contained a range of exactly 2 g. The categories are identified on the x-axis. Vertical bars describe how many observations fall in each category. In Figure 2, the bar in the category labeled 24 indicates that there were seven observations of fish with weights of 24 or 25 grams.

Normal curves are handy because many things in nature tend to have a normal distribution. They are also great because they can be described with only two numbers, the mean and variance. The mean, or average, describes the center of the curve. You can think of it as the balance point. The variance describes the spread of the curve. Is the curve tall with short, stumpy "tails" (the ends of the curve) or is it very flat with long, delicate tails? If you know that something is normally distributed, you can summarize a huge amount of information by simply reporting the mean and the variance.

We use information from the sample to estimate the population mean and variance. We estimate the center, or mean, of the population by calculating the average of our sample data. The variance of the population is reflected in the variability of the sample data. Data from populations with a high variance, long tails, will be more spread out than data from a distribution with a smaller variance, shorter tails. We can use the variability in the sample data to estimate the variance of the population. With an estimate of the variance and an estimate of the mean we know everything we need to know to answer basic questions about the population. For example, what is the population average? Or, What are the odds of extreme observations? A good review of means, variance, and summarizing variability can be found in Gonick and Smith (1993, 7–26).

Sampling Variability

In the Faux Fish Figuring lesson (Day 25), students learn about the sampling distribution of the mean. A more formal description of the ideas in this lesson can be found in Gonick and Smith, pages 104–109, and Zar, pages 83–88.

The sampling distribution of the mean refers to the different estimates of the population mean that are derived from different samples. It is the basis for many types of statistical testing. The most important thing to realize is that when you take a sample of observations the mean or the average of that sample is a random variable—it won't come out the same way every time you take a sample. If you take 10 observations of tree height in a park containing 200 trees and then take an average of your observations, you'll get some number that describes what you think is the average tree height in that park. If you took 10 different tree heights and calculated a new average, you would have a slightly different number. You would then have another estimate of the average tree height in that park. You could, in theory, take 10 tree heights over and over again, calculating the average every time. Most of the time the averages would be about the same and pretty close to the true average of all 200 trees. Sometimes, by chance, you would get 10 particularly small trees and you would calculate an average that's way too small. Once in a while, by the same logic, you would get an average that's way too big.

Faux Fish Figuring (Day 25) demonstrates that the average is a random number and it teaches a few properties of averages. There are two principles involved. The first principle is that the distribution of the average is normal. In other words, if you make a bar graph of all the averages of 10 tree heights in the above example, it would have a bell shape. The second principle about sampling variability of averages is really helpful. It's something we all know by intuition. As you make more and more observations, your estimated average is more and more likely to be close to the truth. If you make three observations of student heights from your class, it would be pretty easy to get three particularly tall or particularly short people. Your average could easily be far from the truth. If you make 10 observations of students in your class, it would be very unusual to have picked 10 particularly short or particularly tall students. You would not expect the average to be very far from the truth. The mathematical way of stating this phenomenon is that the variance of the mean goes down as the sample size goes up.

In the Faux Fish Figuring lesson (Day 25), students start with an ocean of fish, take a sample of three observations, and calculate the average. When all the students plot their average on the class graph, they will see a bell-shaped curve with fairly long tails. Most of the averages are centered around the true population mean (you can identify the true mean or average of the population on the bar graph), but some of the averages will be out in the tails, far from the true population mean. With only three observations, some students will have picked three particularly small or large fish. When the exercise is repeated with samples of 10, the averages will once again have a bell shape but the tails will be much shorter. Overall the 10-sample averages will be much better estimates of the true population mean than the 3-sample averages; the variance of the mean is smaller when the sample size is larger.

Statistical Testing

Statistical testing can be as simple as following a numerical recipe. It's not hard, but it has a reputation for being dull. The way to make it exciting is to explore its underlying ideas. Stat Savvy (Day 26) is a fun lesson designed to build student intuition about statistical concepts. The detailed information presented below is background for the teacher so that he or she can help students understand and appreciate t-tests.

Statistical testing is used to determine whether differences in samples represent differences in the populations from which the samples were drawn. For example, if you had an average of 14 ferns per transect in the sun and an average of 12 ferns per transect in the shade, does that really mean that there are generally different numbers of ferns in the sun versus the shade? In the Faux Fish Figuring lesson (Day 25), students learn that you can get different averages when you take different samples from the same population. In the fern example, perhaps the number of ferns in the shade and the sun is exactly the same but, by chance, you chose some transects in the sun that happened to have a few extra ferns. How can you tell whether the number of ferns is really different in the sun versus the shade?

Statistical testing won't give you the answer. It will give you a probability. Statistical testing will give you the probability of your data having come from the situation described by the null hypothesis. The null hypothesis says that there is no difference between your populations. Stat Savvy (Day 26) starts by demonstrating that even when there is no difference between populations (we took two samples from the exact same population), two samples usually have slightly different averages. Most of the time you would expect two samples from identical populations to be a little bit different but not too much. How can we tell if the two samples are so different that we think they must have come from two different populations (i.e., so different that it is very unlikely that the null hypothesis is true)? Statistical testing will tell you the odds of your two samples being as different as you observed if, in fact, the two populations are the same. In Stat Savvy (Day 26), students uncover the three pieces of information used to evaluate the likelihood of getting a particular set of data if the null hypothesis were true: the difference between the treatment means, the sample size, and the variability of the data. Based on these three pieces of information, students evaluate sample data sets and their own Long-Term Research Project (LTRP) data, summarizing the likelihood that the data come from a situation where the null hypothesis is true as a p-value (defined below).

T-tests are a common statistical test. They give the probability that two populations have the same mean. For example, t-tests can test whether streams are the same temperature as lakes or whether sword ferns are the same height as lady ferns. T-tests are not appropriate for all data but, for purposes of learning, the t-test can be applied to most all student data sets. Mathematically, as well as intuitively, a t-test is based on only three pieces of information: the averages of the two samples, the variability of the two samples, and the number of observations per sample.

It's easy to see why the difference between the two averages is important. If two samples have very different averages they are more likely to come from populations with very different means or centers.

The variability of the samples is also a critical piece of information. If you get two samples that have different averages but very low variability, that tells you a lot more than two samples that have different averages and very high variability. Intuitively, this makes perfect sense. Imagine two samples:

Sample A = 4, 6, 3, 5, 5, 6, 6   and   Sample B = 8, 9, 7, 9, 9, 8, 6

The average of sample A is 5 and the average of sample B is 8. All the observations in sample A are pretty close to 5 and all the observations in sample B are pretty close to 8. Intuitively, it is easy to believe that these samples come from two different populations.

Imagine a different set of samples:

Sample C = 1, 2, 9, 12, 1, 3, 7   and   Sample D = 2, 12, 15, 3, 5, 7, 12

Like samples A and B, sample C has an average of 5 and sample D has an average of 8. But, the spread of the data is different. The data in samples C and D are farther from the average. In other words, the data are more spread out, more variable. In this case, sample C and sample D may come from different populations but the high variance among observations makes it more difficult to determine whether or not this is true. It is easy to imagine that samples C and D came from identical populations but that sample C just happened to get a few more of the smaller numbers.

Sample variability reflects the variance of the populations. If the populations are more spread out (higher variance) then the samples will be more variable. In this case, it is more difficult to detect differences between two populations. In the mathematical calculations for a t-test, information on sample variability is incorporated as the sum of all the squared differences of each observation from the mean (the bottom of columns D and H on the t-test Worksheet, page 147).

Finally, the results of a t-test also depend on the number of items you observe. The reason is demonstrated in Faux Fish Figuring (Day 25). If you observe more items, the average of your sample is more likely to be close to the average of the population. If you observe more items, it is easier to detect differences between two populations if they exist.

When you conduct a t-test, you end up with a t-statistic. To find the p-value, you must look up the t-statistic in a t-table. The t-table and instructions for using it are provided in the practice t-test lesson (Day 27). More information about t-tests can be found in Gonick and Smith (1993, 168–73) or Zar (1984, 126–38).

P-Values

The outcome of a statistical test is presented as a p-value. The p-value is the probability of seeing the observed difference between the two samples if the populations are the same. In other words, the p-value is the probability of getting the data if the null hypothesis is true. A p-value of 0.80 means that there is an 80 percent chance of finding the data when the populations are exactly the same. If you had a p-value of 0.80, you probably wouldn't feel comfortable concluding that the populations are really different. Remember—we start out by assuming that the null hypothesis is true and we only reject that idea when we have strong evidence. With a p-value of 0.80, you would *fail to reject* the null hypothesis; you would continue to assume that the two populations were the same.

A p-value of 0.02 means that there are only 2 in 100 chances of getting samples with such big differences when the populations are really the same. That's pretty strong evidence! With a p-value of 0.02, you could reject the null hypothesis and conclude that the two populations are different.

If you get a p-value of 0.35, what do you conclude? There's only a 35 percent chance of making these observations when the two populations are the same. In science, that is not enough evidence to conclude that the populations are different. What scientists say is, "We cannot reject the null hypothesis based on this evidence." Essentially, that means that we didn't get enough evidence to conclude that the populations are different. It *does not* mean that we proved that the populations are the same. We start out assuming that the null hypothesis is true and that the two populations are the same. We aren't gathering any evidence to prove that; we're trying to gather evidence to disprove it. If we don't gather enough evidence, we *fail to reject* the null hypothesis and we are back in the same boat where we started.

REFERENCES

Gonick, L., and W. Smith. 1993. *The Cartoon Guide to Statistics*. New York: HarperPerennial.
This is an excellent and very inexpensive book. It provides a quick overview of most important concepts in statistics with plenty of humor and great illustrations.

Zar, J. H. 1984. *Biostatistical Analysis*. Englewood Cliffs, NJ: Prentice Hall.
Biostatistical Analysis is the textbook used for many undergraduate and graduate courses in statistics. The examples are oriented toward biology and ecology. It is not a book to sit down and read from cover to cover, but it can be a useful reference if you are interested in the details of particular concepts.

Day 21 — LTRP: Tables Tell the Tale

Overview

I n this lesson, students fill out a Data Collection Notes Worksheet and a Data Table Worksheet. In the Field Report Form, they reflect on their experiences in the field. How would they improve their data collection techniques? What methods had to be adjusted once they started collecting the data? What will they need to remember about particular treatments or about data collected on particular days?

The Data Table helps students to organize their data. On the original data sheets (used on LTRP: Field Trip [Days 19 and 20]), data were recorded in the order in which they were collected in the field. The first step in data analysis is to reorganize the information so that it can be easily interpreted. This exercise will be very simple for some groups and very difficult for others. It's important that it be done carefully because it forms the foundation for the rest of the lessons on data analysis.

Focus Question

How are data organized in a table?

Science Skills

- Students should be able to critique their data collection.
- Students should be able to organize data into a structured table.

Background

For background information describing the concepts in this lesson, see "Record Keeping," page 56.

Materials

- rulers
- graph paper
- Data Collection Notes Worksheet (provided)
- Data Table Worksheet (provided)

Development of Lesson

1. Discuss the field trip or data collection process as a group. What were the positive and negative aspects of the experience? What was frustrating? What were some unexpected

good experiences? What were some unexpected things that groups had to control for? What else affected the data (e.g., weather; equipment being moved overnight)?

2. Ask the students to fill out the Data Collection Notes Worksheet (provided).

3. Once all the students have had a reasonable amount of time to fill out the Worksheet, have the class meet as a group again. If there is time, students can share experiences from their Data Collection Notes Worksheet. Remind students that the comments on their forms will be very helpful when they interpret their results.

4. Have the students look at their data sheets. Explain that the first step in making sense of the data is to organize it. Solicit some suggestions for how to organize the data in a way that helps answer the research question.

5. Go over the Data Table Worksheet as a class, focusing on treatments and replicates. Then have the students make a data table in their LTRP groups. Every student should create a table using a ruler and the group data. The table will have one column for each treatment and one row for each replicate observation. For example, if the project compared water temperature in the lake to water temperature in the stream, there would be one column for lake temperatures and one column for stream temperatures. The rows are for the replicates. If three temperatures were measured in the stream, there would be three rows in the stream column. Some students may have made more than one comparison or they may have different numbers of replicates in each comparison. They can adjust their own tables to describe their particular situation. The last row of the table should be the average of all the replicates in each treatment. This last row can be filled out at the end of Aqueous Averages (Day 22).

Discussion Questions

1. How might the data collection notes that you make now be helpful in interpreting your results later?

2. What is the difference between a treatment and a replicate?

3. Does your data table help you to see patterns in your data? How?

4. Are there any obvious patterns in your data?

5. What other techniques could you use to display your data?

Name _____ Page # _____

Data Collection Notes
Worksheet

1. What parts of your methods, if any, had to be adjusted once you started collecting data? Describe in detail.

_____

_____

_____

_____

2. What was the best thing about collecting data (e.g., methods, equipment, working in a group)? Please describe with details.

_____

_____

_____

_____

3. What thing or things would you change or modify if you were going to do the project again or if you were going to collect more data?

_____

_____

_____

_____

4. Were any of your replicates somehow different from the others? In what way?

_____

_____

_____

_____

5. Were there differences in conditions between days that you collected data or between sets of observations? How might these differences be reflected in your data?

_____

_____

_____

_____

National Science Teachers Association

Data Table Worksheet

The first step in investigating your data is to organize the data as a table.

Research Question: _____

_____

Describe your data—what do the numbers mean (e.g., number of bugs or water temperature)?

_____

_____

This is an example table. There is one column for each treatment and one row for each replicate. There is also a row at the bottom for the average of all replicates in each treatment.

Title of one comparison

Title of the other comparison

	Near the Stream	Far from the Stream
Replicate 1	12	20
Replicate 2	15	24
Replicate 3	9	27
Average of all replicates	12	23.7

The labels of your replicates go in these three boxes

Your data are organized in these middle boxes

Using this table as an example, make a data table of your own data. Use a ruler and pencil so it will be easy to read.

Day 22 — AQUEOUS AVERAGES

Overview

Students begin this lesson by building intuition about averages through redistributing colored water. Students learn that variability does not affect the average of a data set. Students observe the effect of influential data points (particularly high or low data values) on the average of several observations. Finally, the importance of including zeros when calculating an average is demonstrated. Students finish the lesson by completing the data table that was begun in LTRP: Tables Tell the Tale (Day 21) with the average values of all replicate observations for each treatment.

Focus Question

How do different data situations (variability, unusually high or low values, zeros) affect averages?

Science Skills

■ Students should be able to describe the mathematical steps for calculating an average in words.

■ Students should be able to predict how changes in data affect averages.

Materials

■ 6 tall, clear plastic cups or graduated cylinders per student group

■ food coloring

■ water

■ newspaper

■ paper towels

■ 1 tray

■ 1 pitcher

■ colored markers (optional)

■ calculators

■ Averages Worksheet (provided)

Development of Lesson

1. Before the lesson begins, prepare four cups of colored water per group. The cups in each set should be the same color. The water levels in the four cups should range from 1/4 to 3/4 of the cup. The average water level of the four cups should be about 1/2 of the cup. For each set of four cups, prepare a fifth cup of the same color that is nearly full of water. Do not pass out the fifth cup until Step 10. If you have access to enough graduated cylinders, use those instead. Students with graduated cylinders should use calculators to check the results of each experiment. Even if you do not have enough graduated cylinders, you may want to set up a demonstration with graduated cylinders at the front of the room so that students can observe the relationship between pouring water and the mathematical results of calculating an average.

2. Discuss averages as a class. What do students already know? When have they used averages? How will averages help them understand their LTRP data?

3. Divide students into their LTRP groups.

4. Experiment I: Hand out one set of four cups of water to each group and one Averages Worksheet to each student. Ask the students to record the levels of water in the four cups by coloring in the cups on the Worksheet. If graduated cylinders are available, have students record the exact volume of water in each graduated cylinder. Have students guess the average amount of water in the cups by filling in the cup on the Worksheet.

5. Once all the students have recorded their initial conditions, ask the students for suggestions about how to figure out the average amount of water in their four cups (without actually measuring the amount of water in each cup). You may need to push the discussion along. *What is an average? How could you find the "middle" amount of water? What would the mathematical steps tell you to do?* Eventually, students will figure out that the average is the volume of water in any one cup when the water is evenly distributed between all four cups.

6. Have students pour the water between the cups until it is even and record the result on the Worksheet. How close was their guess?

7. Experiment II: Circulate between the groups and redistribute the water between the four cups. This time, make sure that the water is very unevenly distributed, ranging from nearly nothing to nearly full.

8. Discuss the concept of variability as a class. The water in these cups is more variable than the water in the first experiment. How will this affect the average?

9. Have students record the initial conditions, guess the new average, pour water, and record the new average. Students should answer the questions for Experiment II on their Worksheets when they are finished.

10. Experiment III: Have the students redistribute the water in their four original cups so that each cup is different. Hand out a fifth cup of colored water to each group. This cup should be nearly full and the same color of water as the original four cups. Discuss the effect of particularly large or particularly small data values on the average of

several observations. How will this new cup affect the average?

11. Have students record, guess, redistribute, and record as in Experiments I and II. When they have finished, have them answer the questions for Experiment III on the Averages Worksheet.

12. Experiment IV: Ask students if zeros matter when you calculate an average. For example, if you had to calculate the average of 3, 4, 1, 0, and 7, how exactly would you do it?

13. Have the students redistribute the water in the five cups so that each cup is a little bit different. Pass out one empty cup to each group. Tell the students that this new observation is a zero. Have them record, guess, redistribute, and record as in the previous experiments. When they have finished, have them answer the questions for Experiment IV.

14. Clean up the water and divide the students into their LTRP groups. Have them calculate the average of all replicates in each of their treatments. The process should be simple if students work from the data tables that were created in LTRP: Tables Tell the Tale (Day 21). Students should each record their average in the last row of their data tables.

Discussion Questions

1. What other mathematical tools could you use to summarize your data? *Mode and median.*

2. When you report the average for each of your LTRP comparisons, what information are you leaving out? *Variability.* How might this be important?

3. Can two data sets be totally different and still have the same average? Explain your answer.

4. Does any one of your LTRP data points seem to be having a very big effect on your average?

5. How might collecting more samples change the effect of very influential data points?

6. Name some examples where averages are commonly used. *Baseball, grades, weather, car velocity.* Would it be good to know variability in these cases as well? What information about players' abilities, weather, or travel times would you get if you knew about variability instead of just about the average?

7. Are zeros data points? What would happen to your averages if you just ignored them? How could it change the interpretation of your results?

Name _____ Page # _____

Averages Worksheet

EXPERIMENT I:

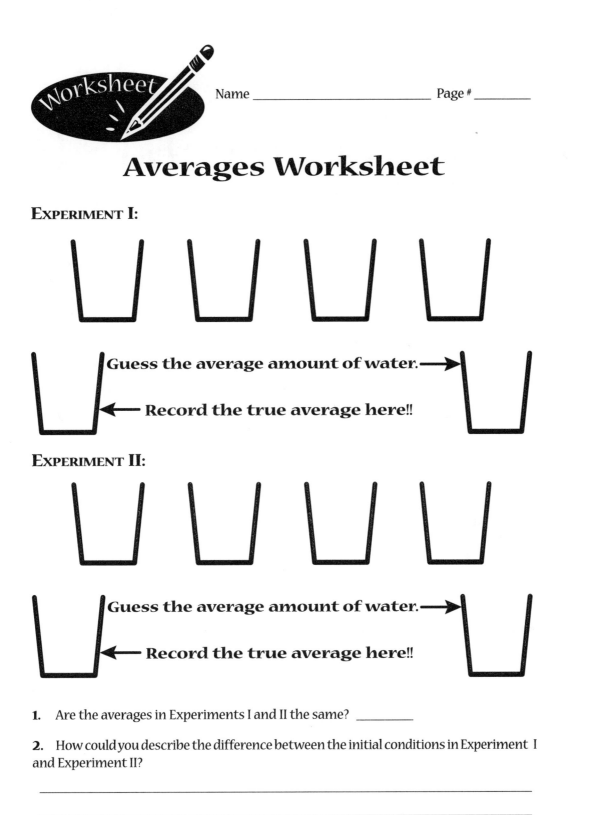

Guess the average amount of water. ➔

⬅ Record the true average here!!

EXPERIMENT II:

Guess the average amount of water. ➔

⬅ Record the true average here!!

1. Are the averages in Experiments I and II the same? _____

2. How could you describe the difference between the initial conditions in Experiment I and Experiment II?

_____

_____

3. When you report the average of several observations, what information are you leaving out?

_____

_____

EXPERIMENT III:

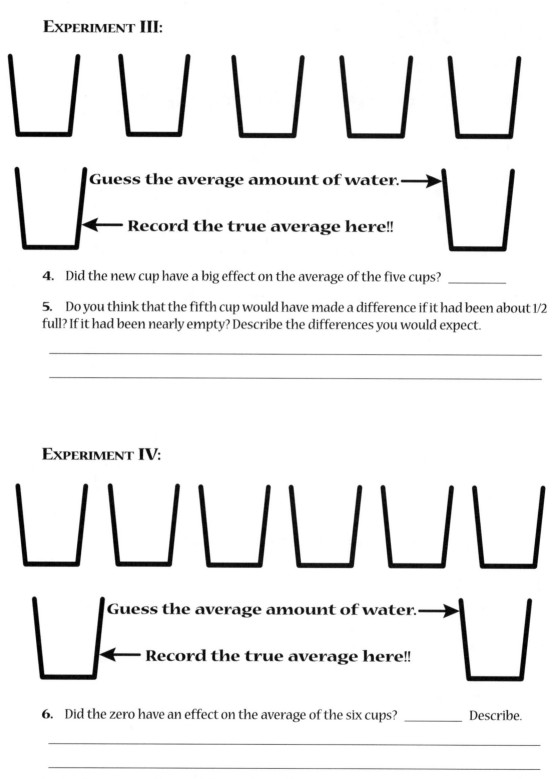

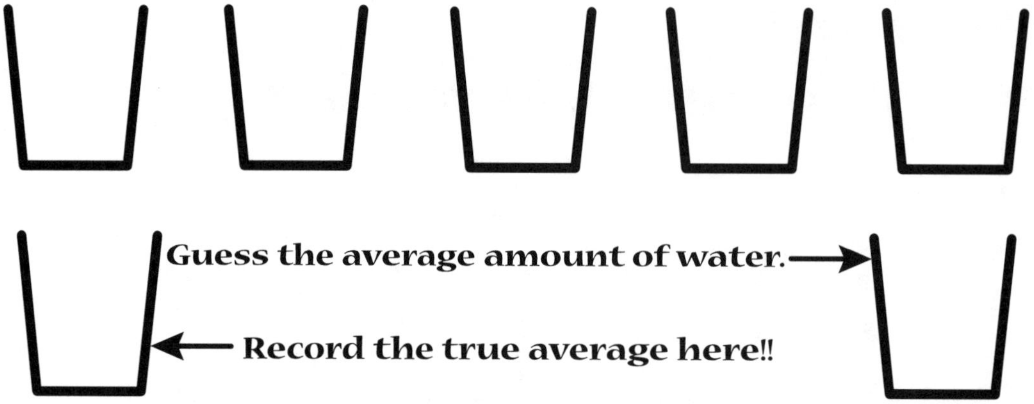
Guess the average amount of water.
Record the true average here!!

4. Did the new cup have a big effect on the average of the five cups? ________

5. Do you think that the fifth cup would have made a difference if it had been about 1/2 full? If it had been nearly empty? Describe the differences you would expect.

____

____

EXPERIMENT IV:

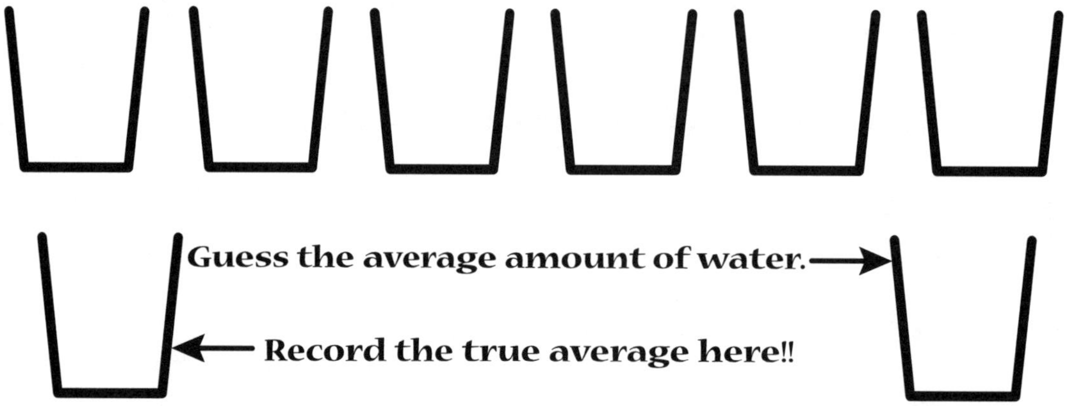
Guess the average amount of water.
Record the true average here!!

6. Did the zero have an effect on the average of the six cups? ________ Describe.

____

____

7. Is the average of 0,0,5,0 different from the average of 0,0,0,5,0?

8. Which average would be smaller? ______________

LTRP: GRAPHING DATA

Days 23, 24

Overview

Students spend the first day inspecting various graphs and figuring out what information the graph communicates about a project and what it leaves out. The discussion focuses on how we use graphs to clearly communicate variability in data and overall trends. The students receive a research scenario from which they create their own graph. The class discusses the strengths of the various graphs produced. The second day, the LTRP groups create graphs of project data.

Focus Question
What information can you learn from a graph?

Science Skills

■ Students should be able to discuss and evaluate research results after reading graphs.

■ Students should be able to recognize variability in data by reading graphs.

■ Students should be able to identify "outliers" by reading various graphs. ("Outliers" are data points that are not like the other data points in a graph. They could indicate a mistake [measurement error, typo] or they could be indicating some important information.)

■ Students should be able to discuss how variability in data can make it difficult to observe a difference between two treatments.

■ Students should be able to create properly labeled graphs from data.

Background
For background information describing the concepts in this lesson, see Wigglin' Worms (Days 13, 14); and Appendix D: How to Make Tables and Graphs Using Microsoft Works. (If you would like your students to create graphs using applications such as Microsoft Works or Excel, you will need to practice this beforehand and make arrangements to use a computer lab, if necessary.)

Materials

- light-colored butcher paper
- dark markers
- 1 copy each of Graphs 1, 2, 3 per student group (provided)
- overhead transparencies of Graphs 1, 2, 3
- 6–10 overhead transparencies, blank or with graph-paper lines copied onto them
- Graphing Data Worksheet (provided)
- Graphing Data Scenario Worksheet (provided)
- rulers
- graph paper
- computer access and disks if students are to do computer graphing of LTRP data

Development of Lesson

1. Tell the class that the next two days will be spent learning how graphs tell stories about research results and how to make graphs that tell the stories well. Put a copy of Graph 1 on the overhead. Survey the class to discover how accustomed they are to reading graphs. What do they know about the research from the graph? Make a list of the information given by the graph. Ask them whether they think this graph does a good job conveying this information. Have them justify their answers. Once you feel that most of the class is comfortable beginning to interpret a graph, divide the class into small groups of approximately four students; these can be their LTRP groups. Give each group copies of Graphs 1, 2, and 3. Give the students 20 minutes to inspect the graphs and answer the questions on the Graphing Data Worksheet.

2. Bring the class together to discuss the three graphs. If needed, you can start by having volunteers answer the Worksheet questions. *Graph 1 presents only the averages of the six replicates. It suggests that there is a difference between the depth that earthworms will burrow in hot and cold conditions. What is missing is the variability in the data and the number of observations. Perhaps there was one worm in cold conditions that burrowed 20 cm (there wasn't), thus having a big effect on the overall average. Scientists need to communicate information about the variability in their data. Graph 2 presents all the data and the averages for each condition, but the presentation is a little misleading. Someone might think that each worm was tested in hot conditions and then tested again in cold conditions. The graph also leads the reader to think more about the individual differences between worms rather than the difference between hot and cold. Finally, there is a glaring omission in Graph 2: the y-axis has no label. We don't know how earthworm depth was measured. Graph 3 includes all the proper labels. It groups the data according to treatment type and it presents all of the data as well as the averages. It would be nice if the averages stood out more from the data. This could be done by using both Graph 1 and Graph 3 in a science research report. Graph 3 also shows that worm 5 in the hot treatment is very different from the other worms. Can this be considered an outlier? What might have influenced this result?* Move the discussion toward the questions "Which graph

best presents the research data? Why?" On the board or overhead, begin a list of the basic parts of a graph. This list must include: title, x-axis units and labels, y-axis units and labels, data, and, if necessary, a key.

3. Now that the students have evaluated sample graphs, have them make their own graphs using the scenario on the Graphing Data Scenario Worksheet. You may want to post the graphs they produce or have them draw graphs on overhead transparencies. Have each group describe their graph to the class and explain why they chose to do things as they did. Help the students point out any confusion in reading the graphs or any parts that were omitted.

4. On the second day of the lesson, begin by reviewing the basic parts of a graph. Then ask the LTRP groups to produce graphs of their research projects. These should be carefully done so they can be used on the posters (Days 34–36). Discuss with the students how they can make their graphs look professional. Discuss using rulers for straight lines, different colors for the different treatments, careful lettering, and lettering size (not too big or too small).

    Note: See Appendix D if you wish to do computer graphing with your students. This takes some preparation. You can expect to do a lot of troubleshooting with the students as they do their graphs. You must be familiar with the graphing software available so you can help troubleshoot. Often, there are several students in the class who already know how to do this and can help their peers.

Discussion Questions

1. Describe the purpose of a graph.

2. Why is it important to graph all of the data collected?

3. Does having more replicates affect the variability in the data? *Having more replicates doesn't change the variability of the data. When you have more replicates, you are more sure of your average even when the data is very variable.*

4. How can you identify an outlier? How might an outlier affect your conclusions? How can you reduce the influence of an outlier on a data set?

5. What are the basic parts that every graph should have?

6. Why do scientists report results of experiments in tables, graphs, and paragraphs?

7. When might you use other kinds of graphs, such as line graphs or pie charts? What other kinds of graphs have you seen? *Line graphs are generally used to describe something changing over time, such as temperature or height. Pie charts are generally used to describe the way things are divided into parts (e.g., the fraction of collected invertebrates that are mosquitoes, potato bugs, worms, and snails).*

8. What kinds of things can you do to make your graph fun to read?

Graph 1

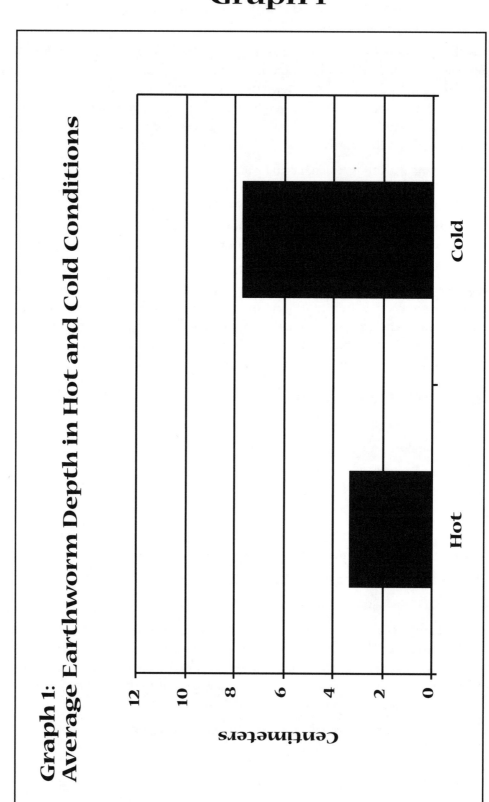

Graph 1:
Average Earthworm Depth in Hot and Cold Conditions

Graph 2

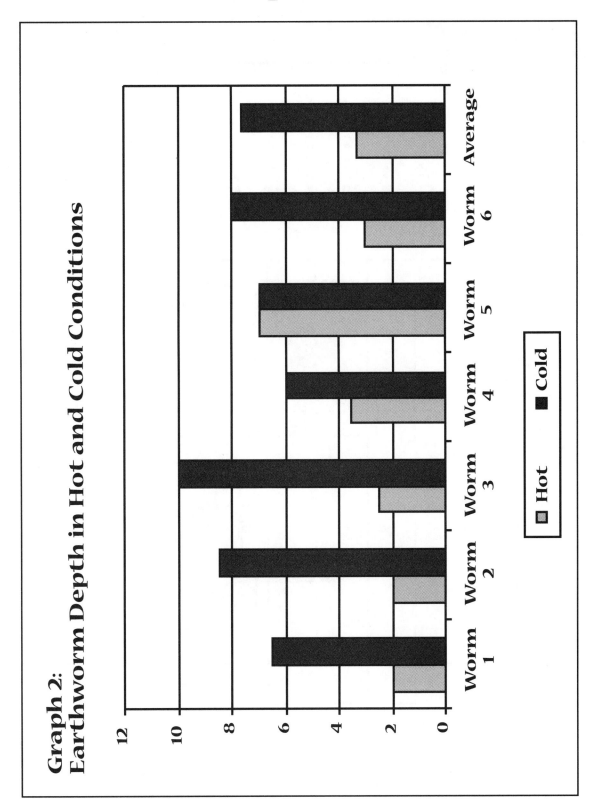

Graph 2:
Earthworm Depth in Hot and Cold Conditions

■ Hot   ■ Cold

Graph 3

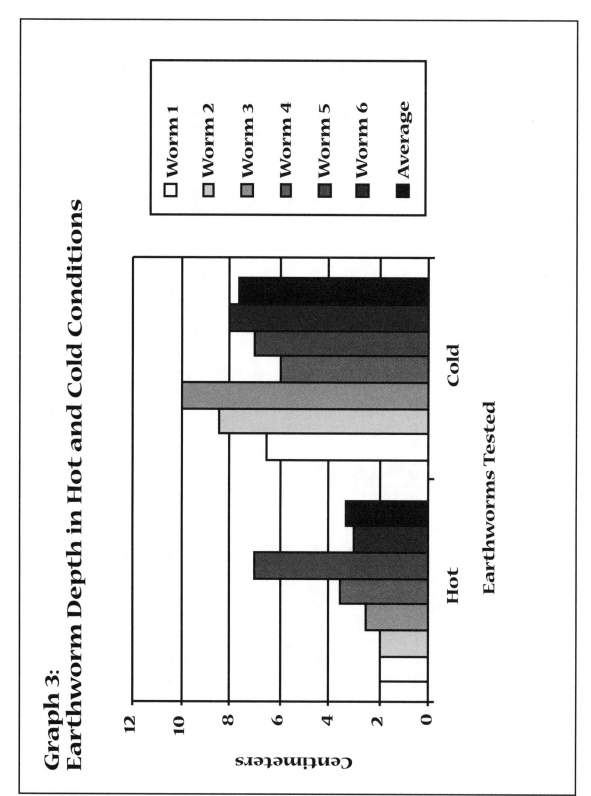

Graph 3:
Earthworm Depth in Hot and Cold Conditions

Name _____ Page # _____

Graphing Data Worksheet

What is the research question that best fits the data presented in all three graphs?

_____

_____

GRAPH 1

1. How is Graph 1 different from Graph 2 and from Graph 3?

_____

_____

_____

2. Does Graph 1 help you answer the research question? Why or why not? If so, what do you think the answer is?

_____

_____

_____

GRAPH 2

1. How is Graph 2 different from Graph 3?

_____

_____

_____

2. Does Graph 2 help you answer the research question? Why or why not? If so, what do you think the answer is?

_____

_____

_____

3. Why do you think the results for worm 5 are the same in both hot and cold conditions?

_____

_____

_____

The Truth about Science

GRAPH 3

1. What do you like best about Graph 3?

_____

_____

_____

2. Does Graph 3 help you answer the research question? Why or why not? If so, what do you think the answer is?

_____

_____

_____

3. How does the variability in the results, especially worm 5, affect your conclusions?

_____

_____

_____

Summary Questions

Which graph *best* communicates the results of the experiment? Why?

_____

_____

_____

List the parts of a graph that should be on every graph.

_____

_____

_____

Graphing Data Scenario Worksheet

Tyson, Lily, Roberto, and Taricha wanted to find out if squirrels preferred walnuts or acorns. At school, they organized their materials. Each student had two plastic trays, 10 walnuts, and 10 acorns. On the day of the experiment, they each went to their own houses after school and took their materials with them. At 5:00 p.m., they began the experiment. They each put the acorns on one tray and the walnuts on the other and they placed the trays 1 m apart. They watched for squirrels to come feed. Each student watched for 20 minutes or until one kind of nut was finished. The next day at school, they made a table to combine their data.

Trials	# of walnuts eaten	# of acorns eaten
1. (Tyson)	1	4
2. (Lily)	3	7
3. (Roberto)	0	3
4. (Taricha)	4	6
Average		

Graph their research data. What do you conclude about squirrel food preferences? Remember to include all the basic parts of a graph. Be neat so others can easily read your graph!

Practice describing your graph with your partner. You may have to present your graph to the class.

Overview

The purpose of this lesson is for the students to learn about normal curves, sampling, and variability. The advantage of using faux fish over real data is that students will know everything about the population of fish from which they are sampling. They can compare the information they get from different sizes of samples to the truth. Sampling theory has been developed by testing techniques in fake situations like this, also called simulations, where the truth is known. Scientists and statisticians apply what they have learned about sampling to situations where the truth is unknown. When actually conducting research, scientists never have the luxury of knowing about the whole population of what they are sampling. This lesson will be referred to repeatedly in the following lessons on statistical testing.

Focus Questions

What can you learn from a sample? How does sample size affect the accuracy of estimates about the population?

Science Skills

■ Students should be able to distinguish between samples and populations.

■ Students should be able to state the basic properties of a normal distribution.

■ Students should be able to state that a sample average can estimate the true average of a population but that it does not estimate this perfectly.

■ Students should be able to explain why samples with more observations provide better estimates of the true population average than samples with fewer observations.

Background

For background information describing the concepts in this lesson, see "Hypothesis versus Null Hypothesis," page 4; "Treatment Types," page 53; "Sampling from a Population," page 45; "The Normal Distribution," page 96; "Sampling Variability," page 98; and "Statistical Testing," page 99.

Materials

■ 1 envelope per student pair

■ 1 pair of scissors per student pair

- butcher paper or overhead transparencies to display class graphs
- handout: 1 Wild Chinook Salmon Bar Graph (Histogram) (of wild chinook salmon weight in grams) per student pair (provided)
- Faux Fish Figuring Worksheet (provided)

Development of Lesson

1. Before the class begins, prepare two graphs at the front of the room. Label one graph "3-Observation Averages" and the other graph "10-Observation Averages." The graphs will eventually be bar graphs of student averages, so the x-axes of both graphs should have the same range as the x-axis of the Wild Chinook Salmon Bar Graph. It will be easiest if you include all the numbers from 16–40 centered between small lines delineating their place so that students can clearly identify the area above, for example, the number 25. The y-axes of both graphs should go from 0 to about 2/3 the number of students in the class. You can use large pieces of butcher paper or overhead transparencies.

2. Discuss normal curves as a class (refer to Background Information above, especially The Normal Distribution, page 96). The basic points that should be covered include the following:

   - The normal curve can describe many things found in nature (heights, weights, etc.).
   - The center or balance point of the normal curve is the average.
   - The spread of the curve describes the variance.

   Compare two normal curves—one with a small variance and one with a large variance. How are they similar? Different? Would they have the same average? How might data from a population with very little variability differ from data from a population with high variability?

3. Explain to the class the difference between a population and a sample. Solicit examples of the population versus the sample from a variety of LTRP projects. Tell the students that in today's class, they will discover what samples can tell you about a population. Understanding samples will help students use their data to answer their LTRP research question. It will help the students to imagine sampling if they remember that their LTRP data probably come from a normal distribution—most things in their population have a value near the average but some are particularly large or small.

4. Hand out the salmon bar graph (one to each pair of students). These fish come from a normal distribution but with only 97 fish, it doesn't look smooth. Discuss as a class what information is contained in the bar graph (numbers of different weights of fish in the population, the mean of the population, the spread or variance of the population). Are there many extreme data values—really small or large fish? The average weight of fish in this population is 29 grams. Are most fish close to the average? Tell the class to imagine that this is the population of all wild chinook in the ocean. They know the weights of every single fish.

The Truth about Science

121

5. Have the students work in pairs to cut out all the fish and put them in an envelope. It will make the process go much faster if they cut the fish in rows or columns first and then snip off the fish. Of course, the fish won't be cut out along the lines; they'll just be on squares of paper.

6. Hand out the Faux Fish Figuring Worksheet. Tell the students that they are going to test how well sampling works. They know the real average of the population (29 grams). Have each student take a sample of three fish from the envelope and calculate the average of the three weights. Each student in the pair should calculate his or her own average from his or her own 3-observation sample. There should be one 3-observation average from each student on the class graph. (If the class has fewer than 30 students, have each student calculate and graph two 3-observation averages.)

7. As each student finishes, have the student graph the 3-observation average on the 3-observation class graph at the front of the room. To graph the average, the student will make a box, 1 unit tall, at the correct location on the x-axis. If, for example, many students have an average of 25, there should be a stack of boxes over the number 25. The stack of boxes will be as high as the number of students with that average. It can be fun to have the students write their initials in the box. The initials can help identify students who haven't added their average to the graph or students who put the 3 and 10 sample average on the same axes by mistake. The final graph will be a histogram of the averages of all the students in the class and will probably have a general bell-shaped or normal distribution.

8. Repeat the exercise with a sample of 10 fish. Have the students graph their 10-observation average on the 10-observation graph at the front of the room. (If the class has fewer than 30 students, have each student calculate two 10-observation averages.)

9. Discuss the results of the activity as a class. What is the difference between the two graphs? Point out that, in both cases, the average of several observations was different from sample to sample—even though the population was exactly the same. Point out that the averages form a normal curve—most averages fall toward the center of the graph (near the true average) but a few are in the tails. What does that tell you about a sample? What does a sample tell you about the population? Is the average of a sample always a perfect estimate of the average of the population? Is it usually pretty good? Can it be off sometimes? What is the difference between a sample of 3 observations and a sample of 10 observations? Which is more variable? What does that tell you about the LTRP? What would happen if you could collect more data? What would a graph of a 25-observation sample look like?

10. The two most important concepts for the students to understand are (1) more samples give you a better estimate of what the population average really is (you are much less likely to get all unusually large or unusually small data points) and (2) two samples from the same population will usually have two somewhat different averages. When flipped around, the second part means that if you have different averages for the two treatments of the LTRP project, it doesn't necessarily mean that the populations are different. Even if the null hypothesis is true, you will get slightly different values for the average of observations in each treatment. This second concept will be rein-

forced in Stat Savvy (Day 26). Save lots of time for the discussion questions! You may also want to save the class graphs for reference in Stat Savvy (Day 26).

Discussion Questions

1. What happens to your estimate of the population average as you make more and more observations?

2. What would happen to your estimate of the population average if you were taking observations from a population that was really variable? From a population that had almost no variability?

3. Why might it be helpful to know that the averages have a normal distribution? *You know that the averages of most samples fall toward the center (the true population average) and only a few are too small or too large.*

4. If you could take a sample of 100 measurements of student height at your school, would it be a perfect estimate of the true average student height? *No, but it would be better than a sample of 50 observations.*

5. Since two samples that look different can come from the same population, how can you tell if the samples come from different populations? What information would go into your decision rule? *The difference between the two averages, variability of replicate observations, the number of observations in your sample.*

6. There are 97 fish in the ocean that you sampled in today's lesson. How many do you think you would have to sample to get a really good estimate of the true population average?

7. How many replicates did you have for each treatment in your LTRP? How reliable do you think your sample average is as an estimate of the truth? Would your answer change if your replicate observations were less variable? More variable?

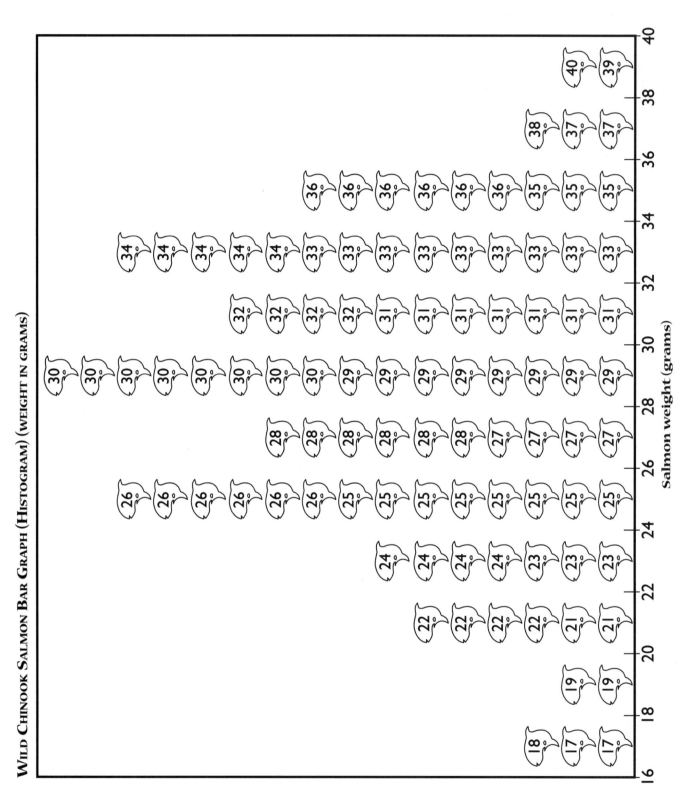

WILD CHINOOK SALMON BAR GRAPH (HISTOGRAM) (WEIGHT IN GRAMS)

Salmon weight (grams)

Faux Fish Figuring Worksheet

The purpose of this lesson is to get a feeling for how well you can estimate things about a population by taking a sample from it.

In your envelope, you have a population of 97 fish. The average weight of these 97 fish is 29 grams. You are a scientist and you want to estimate the average weight of fish in the envelope. You only get to sample 3 fish. Do you think that you will accurately estimate the average of the whole population from a sample of 3 fish? Try it!

EXPERIMENT 1:

Fish 1 Weight _____

Fish 2 Weight _____

Fish 3 Weight _____

Average Fish Weight _____

Was it close to the true average weight of 29 grams? Record your 3-observation average on the class graph.

Would more observations help? Try it with 10 fish!

EXPERIMENT 2:

Fish 1 Weight _____

Fish 2 Weight _____

Fish 3 Weight _____

Fish 4 Weight _____

Fish 5 Weight _____

Fish 6 Weight _____

Fish 7 Weight _____

Fish 8 Weight _____

Fish 9 Weight _____

Fish 10 Weight _____

Average fish weight _____. Record it on the class 10-observation graph.

What do you conclude about sampling? How accurate is it for estimating something about the population? How does sample size affect the accuracy of your estimate?

_____

_____

_____

Day 26 — STAT SAVVY

Overview

In the first part of this lesson, students discuss an example research project as a group and discover that they already have a solid base of intuition about statistics, about the kinds of information used to decide whether the null hypothesis might be true. When evaluating data from two different treatments, the student-scientist needs to consider the difference between the data averages for the two treatments, the number of observations made for each treatment, and the variability of the data observed for each treatment.

In the second part of the lesson, these concepts are reinforced as students evaluate and discuss sample data sets. Concepts from Section II: Experimental Design are reinforced as students imagine what questions they would like to ask the (imaginary) students who collected the sample data sets. Experience asking insightful questions will be important when students are audience members during the oral presentations of other groups. Statistical concepts developed in this lesson form the foundation for the lessons on statistical testing. These concepts and the third worksheet in this lesson can also be used to guide students in critically evaluating their own data in the absence of the formal statistical tests conducted on Day 27.

Focus Question

What information do you use to decide whether two treatments are the same (i.e., whether the null hypothesis is true)?

Background

For background information describing the concepts in this lesson, see "Sampling from a Population," page 95; "Sampling Variability," page 98; "Statistical Testing," page 99; "Treatment Types," page 53; and "Hypothesis versus Null Hypothesis," page 4.

Science Skills

- Students should be able to identify the three pieces of information used to compare data from two different treatments.

- Students should be able to evaluate sample data sets qualitatively.

- Students should be able to ask questions to evaluate research data.

Materials

- 2 envelopes

- Turtle Speed Data (provided)

- Turtle Speed Bar Graphs (provided); these should be made into a transparency

- Stat Savvy Worksheet #1, Stat Savvy Worksheet #2, Stat Savvy Worksheet #3 (provided)

Development of Lesson

1. Prepare two envelopes, one labeled "uphill" and the other "downhill." Photocopy the Turtle Speed Data (page 130). Cut out the numbers and randomly put half of the numbers in the "uphill" envelope and the other half in the "downhill" envelope. Make an overhead transparency of the uphill and downhill turtle speed bar graphs. The transparency can be cut in half so that the two graphs can be set on top of one another.

2. Begin by asking the students how they plan to use their data to decide whether the null hypothesis can be proved false. How can they use their data to decide whether there is a difference between the two treatments? Record the suggestions. You can refer back to these suggestions at the end of the class to determine which still seem like good ideas.

3. Describe the following sample research project. A group of students wants to find out whether the speed of a turtle is greater going uphill or downhill. Have the class state the null hypothesis. Talk about the ways you might collect the data. What would you need to control for? What questions would you want to ask students who reported data on this research topic? For example, did they make all the measurements on one turtle? Was there only one species of turtle involved? Was it the same steepness uphill and downhill? Was it slippery? This type of questioning will help the students critique and evaluate their own project, complete the LTRP: Peer Review lesson on Day 33, and ask good questions of other groups during the oral presentations.

4. As a class, draw five uphill and five downhill observations from the envelopes and calculate the average value for each treatment. Ask the students whether they believe that these data provide evidence that the null hypothesis is not true. Point out that the two average values are different. Ask whether you would expect the average values to be different when the null hypothesis is true. Consider the results from the Faux Fish Figuring exercise.

5. Tell the students that a group of scientists at a nearby university has timed the uphill and downhill speeds of 1,000 turtles. We can consider this the truth, or the population of all possible uphill and downhill speeds. We can use this truth to see if the conclusions from the smaller student project are correct. Place the two graphs side by side or on top of each other on the overhead projector. Is there a difference between turtle travel speeds going uphill and downhill? Tell the class that these are the data from which they sampled. The populations are exactly the same but the sample aver-

ages are different. Discuss why this might happen. For example, just by chance, you might get a particularly fast or slow turtle.

6. This provides scientists with a conundrum. You are going to get different averages for your treatments when the null hypothesis is false *and* when it is true. The science of statistics was developed to answer the question "If the null hypothesis is true, how likely would we be to get these data?" As a class, define a p-value. A p-value (or probability value) summarizes the chance of getting your data if the null hypothesis is true.

7. How do you summarize "data like this" into one meaningful number so you can calculate the probability value? There are formal mathematical ways to summarize data and calculate a p-value. Students already have a lot of intuition about what information goes into those summaries and mathematical tests. Ask the students what qualities of a data set might be important. *The qualities are (1) the difference between the sample averages, (2) the number of samples, and (3) the variability of the data.* Discuss why each of these three pieces of information is important in determining the strength of the evidence that the null hypothesis is false. (It may help for the students to look first at the Faux Fish Figuring class graphs before trying to arrive at the three-part answer.)

8. In the second half of the lesson, students have the opportunity to evaluate several examples of research projects and data sets as well as their own LTRP data. Hand out the three Worksheets (Stat Savvy Worksheet #1, Stat Savvy Worksheet #2, and Stat Savvy Worksheet #3), and let students puzzle in pairs or in small groups over the example data sets in the first two Worksheets. What do they conclude for each data set? Have them estimate a p-value for each one. They can write a p-value as a percent, an odds (50/50), a chance (1 in a million), or any other description of their concept of the likelihood of the data if the null hypothesis were true. (It may help to hand out one Worksheet at a time. Some groups may not be ready for the more difficult questions on Worksheet #2. The difficult questions are an opportunity for those students interested in an extra challenge to discuss and share their ideas with the class. Students will need access to their LTRP data tables and LTRP graphs to complete the third Worksheet.)

9. Meet again as a class and compare results. It can be fun to graph the estimated p-values for each data set. Did most groups estimate similar values? Have students defend their estimates. You may choose to reveal the true p-values or not. Encourage the students to question the methods as well as the final data. Spend as much time as possible brainstorming important questions to ask each fictional research group.

Note: There are many possible structures that make this lesson fun and interactive. You might give half the class Worksheet #1 and half the class Worksheet #2 and then have them present their results to each other in small groups. Or, one representative of each group might present the answer to one question to the whole class. It is not important that all students complete Worksheets #1 and #2 on sample data. It *is* important that all students complete Worksheet #3 on their LTRP data. An excellent way to encourage independent thinking and critical debate is to have students complete Worksheet #3 independently and then meet in their LTRP groups to share their opinions. Worksheet #3 is also a good opportunity for LTRP groups to share results with the class for feedback and ideas.

P-values for Sample Data Experiments:

Experiment #1 = 0.05

Experiment #2 = 0.88; Question #4, p-value = 0.0001

Discussion Questions

1. Explain why we always set up a null hypothesis the way we do.

2. If variance makes it difficult to understand your data, how might you be able to re-duce the variance? *Control for more factors, make more careful measurements, ask a more limited question.*

3. How many replicates did you have for each treatment in your LTRP? How reliable do you think your sample average is as an estimate of the truth? Do you think your LTRP conclusion would change if you collected more data? Would your answer change if your replicate observations were less variable? More variable?

4. Think back to your favorite advertising campaign. Do advertisements that claim to provide research results usually tell you all three pieces of information (the difference between sample averages, the number of samples, and the variability of the data)? How can advertisers mislead people by not including some or all of this information? Think of a few ways in which simply stating averages could be misleading. Can you think of any specific advertising campaigns that might be playing this game?

Turtle Speed Data

			0.8	1.0	0.8
1.1	1.2	1.0	0.4	0.9	0.6
0.9	0.9	1.1	0.8	0.9	0.7
0.7	0.7	0.8	1.0	0.6	0.9
0.5	0.6	1.1	0.7	1.0	1.0
0.9	0.9	0.8	1.0	1.4	1.1
1.2	0.7	0.8	1.1	1.1	0.7
0.7	1.2	0.8	1.1	0.8	1.0
0.9	0.9	0.9	1.1	0.9	1.0
0.7	0.8	1.0	0.7	0.7	0.5
0.7	0.6	1.0	0.8	0.8	1.0
1.1	0.9	0.7	0.8	0.8	0.9
1.0	1.1	0.9	0.9	0.8	1.1

National Science Teachers Association

Turtle Speed Bar Graphs

Uphill Speeds

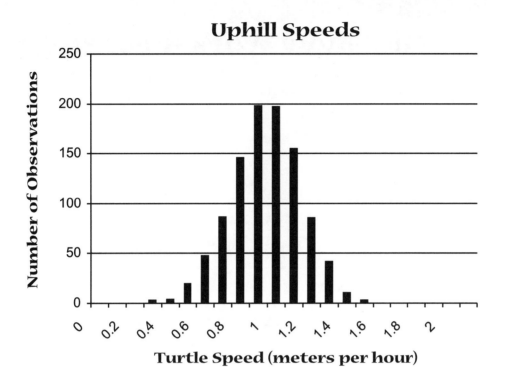

Downhill Speeds

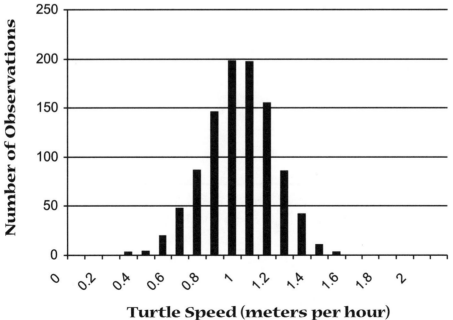

Name _____ Page # _____

Stat Savvy Worksheet #1

Experiment #1: A group of students measured the number of insects in flowering versus nonflowering shrubs. They took eight samples from each type of shrub. Their data look like this (number of insects):

Flowering Shrubs	Nonflowering Shrubs
7	2
6	5
9	9
2	2
14	7
11	4
11	8
9	5
Avg. = 8.23	**Avg. = 5.25**

1. State the null hypothesis. Do you think the null hypothesis is true?

    _____

    _____

2. What would you conclude about insects and shrubs if this were your research project? What about the data did you consider to make your decision?

    _____

    _____

    _____

3. If there really were no difference between the number of insects in the two kinds of shrubs, could you get these data just by chance?   **Yes**   **No**

4. If the null hypothesis were true, how likely would you be to get data like these?

    _____

    _____

    _____

5. Discuss the methods you would have to use to do this experiment. If you wanted to know more about this data, what questions would you want to ask the researchers?

    _____

    _____

    _____

    _____

National Science Teachers Association

Stat Savvy Worksheet #2

Experiment #2: A group of students were interested in mushroom growth. They wanted to know if mushrooms grew taller in the sun or in the shade. The following data describe their results. Data are graphed on page 135.

Heights in the sun (cm): 7.0, 7.4, 6.5, 6.7, 5.0, 7.0, 6.4, 8.1, 7.1, 7.5, 6.9, 6.5, 6.0, 8.0, 6.6, 8.7, 5.4, 7.2, 5.8, 5.4, 6.2, 6.0, 7.6, 6.3, 5.5, 8.2, 6.0, 7.3, 7.7, 6.5, 6.7, 7.9, 7.7, 7.0, 5.4, 7.1, 7.6, 7.3, 7.4, 8.3, 6.5, 8.1, 6.7, 9.0, 7.2, 7.4, 7.6, 6.1, 6.3, 8.3, 7.6, 7.3, 8.4, 7.8, 5.8, 7.5, 7.3, 7.5, 6.0   AVERAGE = 7.0

Heights in the shade (cm): 5.7, 4.7, 16.8, 7.3, 7.2, 7.7, 20.1, 5.8, 7.1, 4.9, 5.3, 4.3, 4.2, 5.0, 5.2, 3.9, 5.4, 5.6, 6.1, 5.6, 5.7, 5.6, 7.3, 5.9, 5.8, 5.5, 8.0, 6.9, 8.4, 5.3, 7.7, 4.4, 6.5, 6.9, 7.9, 5.9, 5.5, 6.7, 5.6, 15.2, 4.6, 5.2, 4.5, 5.6, 6.0, 6.0, 5.7, 8.2, 4.3, 5.3, 13.4, 7.4, 4.7, 5.3, 13.1, 6.5, 6.9, 6.6, 15.4, 14.9   AVERAGE = 7.1

1. Do you think there is a difference in mushroom heights between mushrooms in the shade and in the sun? Why or why not (based on the data—numbers and graphs)?

_____

_____

_____

_____

2. If the null hypothesis were true, what would be the odds of getting data like these? Summarize the evidence you used to make this estimate.

_____

_____

_____

_____

3. There are a few very large shade observations. Can you imagine reasons why you might get a few extreme points?

_____

_____

_____

_____

_____

_____

4. If you remove the seven very large observations, the new shade average is 5.9. What do you conclude about the null hypothesis now? Estimate a new p-value.

_____

_____

_____

5. What is your overall conclusion about mushroom heights in the shade and in the sun based on these data? What questions would you want to ask the researchers before you made a final decision?

_____

_____

_____

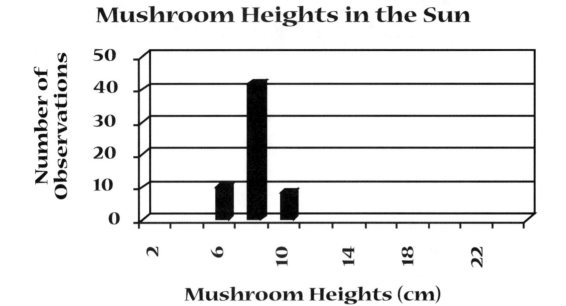

Mushroom Heights in the Sun

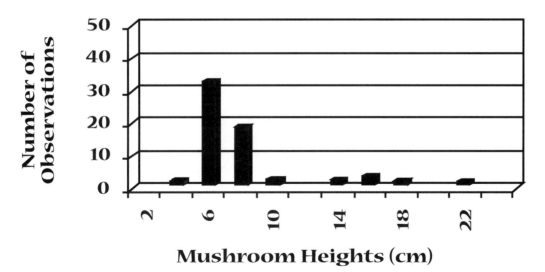

Mushroom Heights in Shade

Stat Savvy Worksheet #3

Experiment #3: Experiment 3 is your LTRP. Get out your data table and your graphs and examine the patterns you see.

1. State your null hypothesis.

   _____

   _____

   _____

   _____

2. What is the difference between your two averages?

   _____

   _____

   _____

3. What is your sample size? How many observations did you make in each treatment?

   _____

   _____

   _____

4. Are your data very variable or, within each treatment, are most observations similar?

   _____

   _____

   _____

5. If the null hypothesis were true, what do you think would be the odds of getting data like this?

   _____

   _____

   _____

6. What one piece of information was the most important in making your estimate?

   _____

   _____

   _____

7. What do you conclude about your topic based on the results of your research?

_____

_____

_____

8. What questions are people likely to ask about your methods or your results? What might be confusing to other people? What parts of your methods might have affected your research results?

_____

_____

_____

_____

_____

_____

_____

_____

_____

_____

_____

_____

_____

Day 27 ———————— T-TEST PRACTICE

Overview

Students learn the basic steps for conducting a t-test. A t-test determines the probability of getting a set of observations if the null hypothesis is true. In this lesson, students practice on simulated data as a class. The group discussion at the beginning of this lesson reviews the concepts from Faux Fish Figuring and Stat Savvy in the context of statistical testing. A handout ("Statistical Testing Background," page 145) also reviews the major ideas. During the t-test calculations, the whole class can walk through the mathematical steps together on group data. The teacher should be familiar with the way the Practice T-Test Worksheet is laid out before the class begins. For this reason, we have provided the Teacher Example Worksheet. It is the same as the Practice T-Test Worksheet but the data are filled in. This lesson will be easier for students who are familiar with square roots, squares, and percentages. Students will be using the same worksheet format in the next lesson, LTRP: T-Tests, Day 28.

Focus Question

How do you calculate a p-value?

Science Skills

■ Students should be able to follow the basic steps in calculating a t-test.

■ Students should be able to read a p-value from a t-table.

■ Students should be able to relate results of statistical tests to the null hypothesis and the hypothesis.

Background

For background information describing the concepts in this lesson, see "Hypothesis versus Null Hypothesis," page 4; "Statistical Testing," page 99; "P-Values," page 101; "Sampling from a Population," page 95; and "Sampling Variability," page 98.

Materials

■ fish in envelope from the Faux Fish Figuring lesson (the fish that were cut out from the Wild Chinook Salmon Bar Graph (Histogram) on page 124)

■ Wild Chinook Salmon (bar graph to be used for overhead transparency; page 143)

■ Hatchery Chinook Salmon (bar graph to be used for overhead transparency; page 142)

- handout: Hatchery Chinook Salmon Bar Graph (Histogram) (provided)
- handout: Statistical Testing Background (provided)
- Teacher Example Worksheet—4 pages (provided)
- Practice T-Test Worksheet—4 pages (provided)
- calculators

Development of Lesson

1. Before the lesson begins, make one copy of the Hatchery Chinook Salmon Bar Graph (Histogram) (page 144). Cut out the individual fish from the copy as for the Faux Fish Figuring lesson and place them in an envelope labeled Hatchery Fish. It will also be important to go over the Teacher Example Worksheet.

2. Review the characteristics of a normal curve. The shape looks like a mound and the average is in the middle. The sides are symmetrical. Tell the students that today they will be comparing wild salmon weights with hatchery salmon weights to see if there is a difference. Write the research question on the overhead. Draw two normal curves on two overhead transparencies and label one "Wild Salmon Weights" and the other "Hatchery Salmon Weights." Ask the students to put the two bar graphs together in a way that represents the null hypothesis of no difference. They should be able to tell you to put the graphs on top of each other. Now ask them how to place the graphs to represent the hypothesis that there is a difference in salmon weights. This time the graphs are placed side by side with only a little overlap. Tell the students that they will be using a test that all scientists use to help them determine the odds of their data if the null hypothesis is true. Usually scientists put all the numbers into a computer and they get a result. Today, the students will be the scientists and the computers.

3. A review of key concepts is outlined in the handout "Statistical Testing Background." The first concept to discuss is the general purpose of statistical testing. The important information is outlined on the front of the handout. The purpose of statistical testing is to decide whether you think the null or the research hypothesis is true. You have to look at your data to make that decision. It might be worth reminding students of what they learned from Faux Fish Figuring (Day 25): (1) the more observations you make, the better the sample average will estimate the population average, (2) different samples from the same population will have different averages, and (3) just because two samples have different averages doesn't mean that the two populations have different averages.

4. On the back of the handout are several important lists. Review what students learned in Stat Savvy (Day 26). Go over this information slowly as a class. Students should discuss how each piece of information used in a t-test might help them make a decision as to whether samples were taken from a situation where the null hypothesis is true. They should also review how they will use a p-value and what kind of conclusions they will be able to make. Emphasize the fact that students will never be able to say, "The null hypothesis is true."

5. Explain to the students that they are going to do an experiment to determine whether hatchery or wild fish are bigger. Have a brief discussion about hatchery versus wild fish. Hatchery fish are raised in a hatchery and are fed fish food every day, but they may not have very good health. Wild fish are from fish that spawn naturally; they must search for their food every day and are usually in good health. Have students fill in their hypotheses on the Practice T-Test Worksheet.

6. As a class, have students take a sample of five fish from the wild fish envelope and a sample of five fish from the hatchery fish envelope. Each student should record the class data in columns A and E of the Practice T-Test Worksheet. (It will be *much* easier if all students record the same data.)

7. Students should fill in the table on the front side of the Worksheet. First, they will need to calculate the average for wild and for hatchery fish and record that at the bottom of columns A and E. The average should be copied into each cell in columns B and F as well. Next, the students will take each observation and subtract the average from it. Students record the difference between each observation and the average for that treatment in columns C and G. These differences should be squared and recorded in columns D and H. Finally, the squared differences are totaled for wild and for hatchery fish and recorded at the bottom of columns D and H.

8. Students have now calculated their Average and their Sum of Squares for both wild and hatchery fish. The Sum of Squares describes the variability in each sample. On the reverse side of the page, students simply fill in the squares to get their t-statistic. (The teacher example may be particularly helpful here.) Notice that all three pieces of information necessary for evaluating the data—difference between the means, sample size, and variability—are used in the calculation.

9. Finally, students look up their p-value on the t-table at the end of the Worksheet and record it in the appropriate box. The final step of the statistical testing is for students to evaluate the meaning of the p-value. What does it tell you about the null hypothesis? Do you still think it's true?

10. In the final discussion, you may want to bring out the original histograms (with all the little fish—page 124 and page 144). Copies of traditional histograms (bar graphs) are also provided for wild and for hatchery fish. Since this was a simulated experiment, students can compare the results of their statistical tests with the truth. At first glance the histograms may look very similar but the axes are different. Are the averages of the two populations really different? What did the information from the p-value tell you? Which population is more variable? How can you tell?

Discussion Questions

1. Why are each of the following pieces of information important in deciding if the null hypothesis is likely to true: the difference between the two sample averages, the variability of the replicates in each sample, and the number of replicates in each sample? *If the sample averages are very far apart, it's less likely that the null hypothesis is true. If there is a lot of variability in the replicates, it will be hard to tell which case is true and so we*

are more likely to stick with our original assumption that the null hypothesis is true. The more observations in a sample, the better the estimate of the population average. If two samples have lots of observations and their averages are still pretty different, it's unlikely that the null hypothesis is true.

2. Why can't you ever prove the null hypothesis?

3. Now that you know something about statistics, why do you think it was important to set up your hypotheses early?

4. What are some examples of other situations where statistics might be useful?

5. What information does a p-value tell you?

6. Why do you think there has to be a different row in the t-table depending on the total number of observations in your two samples?

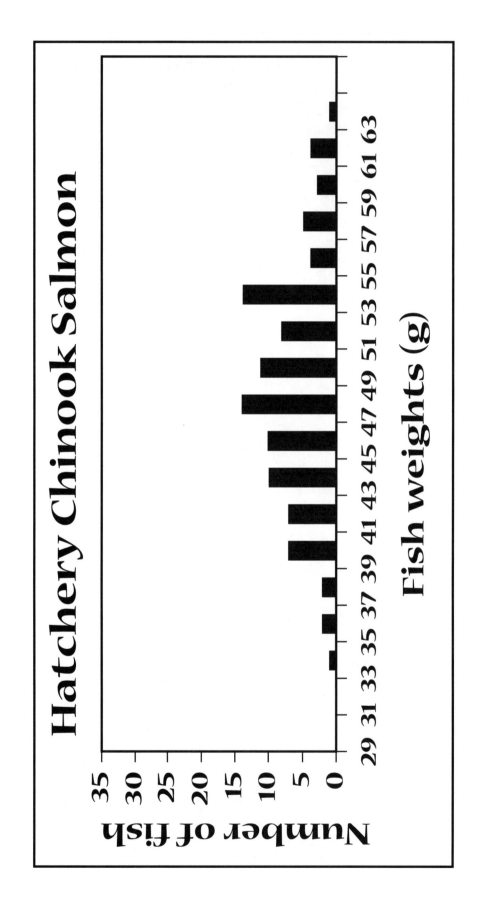

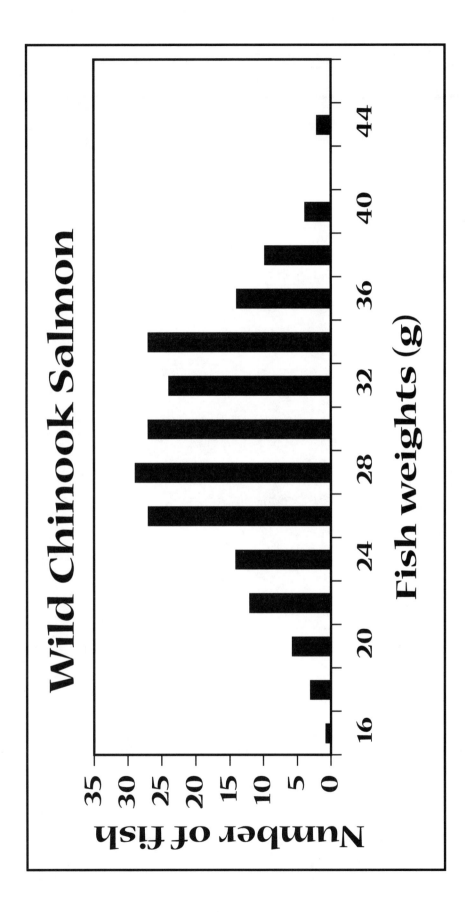

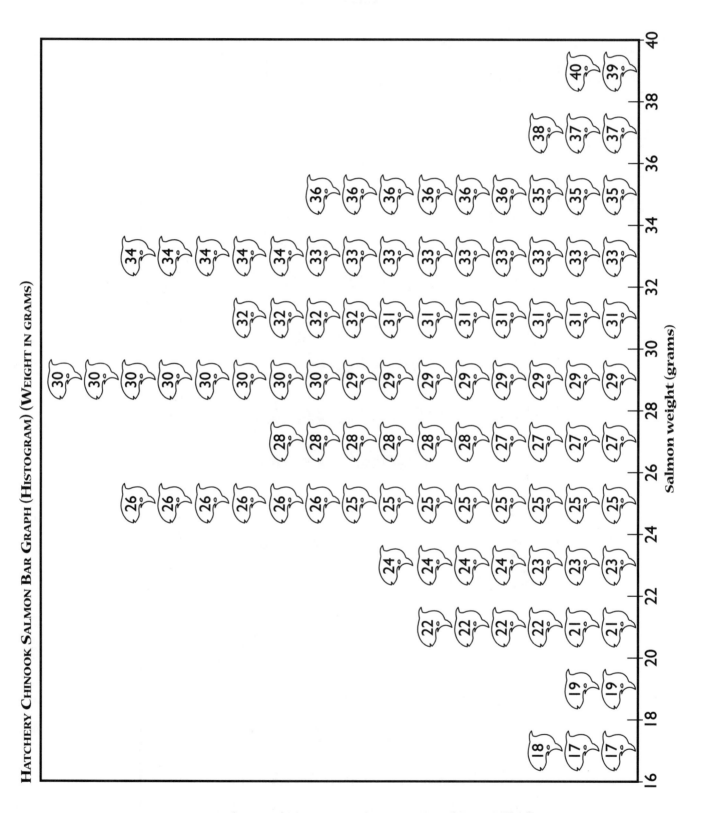

Hatchery Chinook Salmon Bar Graph (Histogram) (Weight in grams)

Salmon weight (grams)

Statistical Testing Background

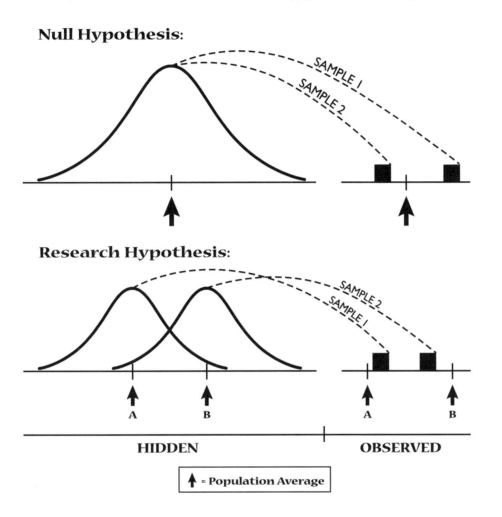

Null Hypothesis:

SAMPLE 1
SAMPLE 2

Research Hypothesis:

SAMPLE 2
SAMPLE 1

A   B

A   B

HIDDEN   **OBSERVED**

↑ = Population Average

When you do research, all you get is what you observe! You try and figure out what the hidden part looks like based on what you observe.

The arrows show the averages of the true distribution for both the hidden and the observed parts. The hidden part for the situation where the null hypothesis is true is one distribution from which two samples have been taken. The hidden part for the situation where the hypothesis is true is two different distributions with two different averages. The observed samples from the two situations look very similar. You must use information from your observed data to decide whether you think the hidden part could look like your null hypothesis or not. If the sample averages are close together, it might be because the null hypothesis is true or it might be because the hypothesis is true. If the two sample averages are very far apart, you can usually conclude that the hypothesis is true. Statistics can tell us the probability of getting our data if the null hypothesis is true. This is the p-value. P stands for probability. You can use the p-value to make your best guess about whether you think the null hypothesis is true.

You can do a t-test to get a p-value. Three pieces of information are used to do the t-test:

1. The difference between the averages for your two treatments.

2. The variability of the observations that go into each average.

3. The number of observations that go into each average.

REMEMBER TWO THINGS:

1. We start out assuming that the null hypothesis is true—that there is no difference between our two treatments.

2. By gathering data, we can develop evidence that the null hypothesis isn't true. The p-value tells us the odds of our null hypothesis being true, given our data.

EVALUATING THE P-VALUE:

Here's how we can make a decision about whether the data come from the null hypothesis or the hypothesis. The t-test can tell us the odds of our data *if* the null hypothesis is true. So, the t-test tells us the odds of getting our data if there is no difference between the two treatments.

A. If the odds of getting our data when the null hypothesis is true are very, very small, we assume that the hypothesis is true. In other words, if the p-value is very small then there is a very small chance of getting this data if there were no difference between the two treatments. So, we *reject* the null hypothesis. Scientists often use a cut-off of 0.05 or 0.1 for rejecting the null hypothesis.

B. If the p-value is not very, very small then we have to stick with our original assumption that the null hypothesis is true. In this case, we *fail to reject* the null hypothesis.

Teacher Example Worksheet

(To the Teacher: This worksheet is identical to the students' Practice T-Test Worksheet on pages 151–154, except that example data have been filled in here.)

Do you think wild chinook salmon are the same size as chinook salmon from a hatchery? We will do a "research" project and a statistical test to see if the size of wild versus hatchery chinook salmon is the same or different.

Null Hypothesis: There is no difference between the size of hatchery and wild chinook salmon.

Hypothesis: There is a difference between the size of hatchery and wild chinook salmon.

The Data: (These will be fish weights in grams when the students do the activity. For now, they are simplified so the steps are easy to follow.)

A	B	C	D	E	F	G	H
Wild Fish	Average	Data - Average (A-B)	Difference Squared C^2	Hatchery Fish	Average	Data - Average (E-F)	Difference Squared G^2
5	6	-1	1	10	11	-1	1
4	6	-2	4	13	11	2	4
7	6	1	1	16	11	5	25
8	6	2	4	8	11	-3	9
6	6	0	0	8	11	-3	9
Wild Average: 6			Total Sum of Squares: 10	Hatchery Average: 11			Total Sum of Squares: 48

Teacher Example Worksheet

(continued)

A couple more things you will need:

Number of Observations of Wild Fish   = $\boxed{5}$ = n_{wild}

Number of Observations of Hatchery Fish   = $\boxed{5}$ = $n_{hatchery}$

Follow the recipe. Think about what information is being incorporated at each step. (You only have to fill in the squares.)

Step 1. Calculate the pooled variance.

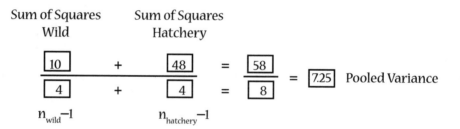

$$\frac{\boxed{10}}{\boxed{4}} \quad + \quad \frac{\boxed{48}}{\boxed{4}} \quad = \quad \frac{\boxed{58}}{\boxed{8}} \quad = \boxed{7.25} \quad \text{Pooled Variance}$$

Sum of Squares Wild · Sum of Squares Hatchery · $n_{wild}-1$ · $n_{hatchery}-1$

Step 2. Calculate UGH. (This number doesn't have a real name but you will need it in Step 3.)

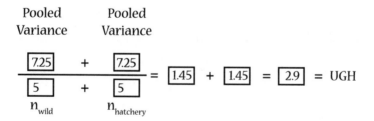

$$\frac{\boxed{7.25}}{\boxed{5}} \quad + \quad \frac{\boxed{7.25}}{\boxed{5}} \quad = \boxed{1.45} + \boxed{1.45} = \boxed{2.9} = \text{UGH}$$

Pooled Variance · Pooled Variance · n_{wild} · $n_{hatchery}$

Step 3.

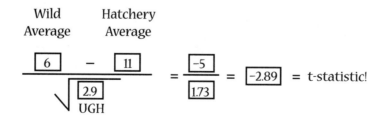

$$\frac{\boxed{6} - \boxed{11}}{\sqrt{\boxed{2.9}}} = \frac{\boxed{-5}}{\boxed{1.73}} = \boxed{-2.89} = \text{t-statistic!}$$

Wild Average · Hatchery Average · UGH

Corrected Version of Step 2, page 148

Teacher Example Worksheet

(continued)

A couple more things you will need:

Number of Observations of Wild Fish $= \boxed{5} = n_{wild}$

Number of Observations of Hatchery Fish $= \boxed{5} = n_{hatchery}$

Follow the recipe. Think about what information is being incorporated at each step. (You only have to fill in the squares.)

Step 1. Calculate the pooled variance.

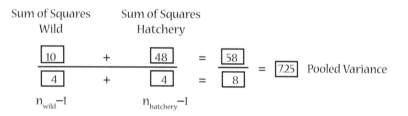

$$\frac{\underset{Wild}{\text{Sum of Squares}}}{n_{wild}-1} + \frac{\underset{Hatchery}{\text{Sum of Squares}}}{n_{hatchery}-1} \quad \frac{\boxed{10} + \boxed{48}}{\boxed{4} + \boxed{4}} = \frac{\boxed{58}}{\boxed{8}} = \boxed{7.25} \text{ Pooled Variance}$$

Step 2. Calculate UGH. (This number doesn't have a real name but you will need it in Step 3.)

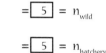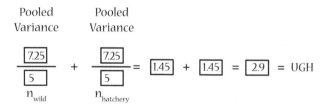

$$\frac{\underset{n_{wild}}{\text{Pooled Variance}}}{\boxed{5}} + \frac{\underset{n_{hatchery}}{\text{Pooled Variance}}}{\boxed{5}} = \boxed{1.45} + \boxed{1.45} = \boxed{2.9} = \text{UGH}$$

with Pooled Variance $= \boxed{7.25}$ in each numerator.

Step 3.

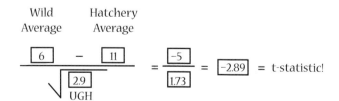

$$\frac{\underset{Wild\ Average}{\boxed{6}} - \underset{Hatchery\ Average}{\boxed{11}}}{\sqrt{\underset{UGH}{\boxed{2.9}}}} = \frac{\boxed{-5}}{\boxed{1.73}} = \boxed{-2.89} = \text{t-statistic!}$$

Teacher Example Worksheet

(continued)

Take a look at the t-table on page 150. You can use it to get a p-value from a t-statistic. Just follow the three steps. (Sometimes it helps to use a ruler and mark the row and column of interest.)

Step 1. Calculate your total number of observations −2. = ⟨8⟩

Step 2. Find the row for your total number of observations − 2.

Step 3. Read across to the number that is closest to your t-statistic ⟨2.89⟩ but not any bigger. If all the numbers in that row are bigger than your t-statistic, go to step 5.

Step 4. Go up to the top of that column and read off your p-value.

Record your p-value: ⟨0.05⟩

Since you stopped at a number that was a little bit smaller than your actual t-statistic, you can say that your p-value is less than that or

$$p < \boxed{0.05}.$$

OK—that means that the odds of the null hypothesis being true are less than ⟨5%⟩.

Step 5. If all the numbers in that row are bigger than your p-value, it means that your p-value is bigger than 0.50. That means that the odds of your null hypothesis being true are greater than ⟨ ⟩.

What do you conclude about your hypotheses? Do you think that your hypothesis is probably true or do you have to keep assuming that your null hypothesis is true?

There is less than a 5 percent chance that our data come from a situation in which the null hypothesis is true. That means that there is less than a 5 percent chance that the size of hatchery and wild fish is the same. That is such a small chance that I can reject the null hypothesis as being too unlikely. I conclude that the research hypothesis is probably true. Hatchery chinook salmon and wild chinook salmon are different sizes.

Teacher Example Worksheet

(continued)

T-TABLE

p-value ⟋ Total Observations–2	0.50	0.20	0.10	0.05	0.02	0.01	0.005	0.002	0.001
1	1.00	3.08	6.31	12.71	31.82	63.66	127.32	318.31	636.62
2	0.82	1.89	2.92	4.30	6.97	9.93	14.09	22.33	31.56
3	0.77	1.64	2.35	3.18	4.54	5.84	7.45	10.22	12.92
4	0.74	1.53	2.13	2.78	3.75	4.60	5.60	7.17	8.61
5	0.73	1.48	2.02	2.57	3.37	4.03	4.77	5.89	6.87
6	0.72	1.44	1.94	2.45	3.14	3.71	4.32	5.21	5.96
7	0.71	1.42	1.90	2.37	3.00	3.50	4.03	4.79	5.41
8	0.71	1.40	1.86	2.31	2.90	3.36	3.83	4.50	5.04
9	0.70	1.38	1.83	2.26	2.82	3.25	3.69	4.30	4.78
10	0.70	1.37	1.81	2.23	2.76	3.17	3.58	4.14	4.59
11 - 15	0.70	1.36	1.80	2.20	2.72	3.11	3.50	4.03	4.44
15 - 20	0.70	1.34	1.75	2.13	2.60	2.95	3.29	3.73	4.07
20 - 50	0.69	1.33	1.73	2.09	2.53	2.85	3.15	3.55	4.85
50 - 100	0.68	1.30	1.68	2.01	2.40	2.68	2.94	3.26	3.50

Practice T-Test Worksheet

Do you think wild chinook salmon are the same size as chinook salmon from a hatchery? We will do a "research" project and a statistical test to see if the size of wild versus hatchery chinook salmon is the same or different.

Research Question:
Are hatchery and wild chinook salmon the same size or different?

Null Hypothesis:

_____

_____

_____

Hypothesis:

_____

_____

_____

The Data

A	B	C	D	E	F	G	H
Wild Fish	Average	Data - Average (A-B)	Difference Squared C^2	Hatchery Fish	Average	Data - Average (E-F)	Difference Squared G^2
Wild Average:			Total Sum of Squares:	Hatchery Average:			Total Sum of Squares:

Name _____ Page # _____

Practice T-Test Worksheet

(continued)

A couple more things you will need:

Number of Observations of Wild Fish = $\boxed{}$ = n_{wild}

Number of Observations of Hatchery Fish = $\boxed{}$ = $n_{hatchery}$

Follow the recipe. Think about what information is being incorporated at each step. (You only have to fill in the squares.)

Step 1. Calculate the pooled variance.

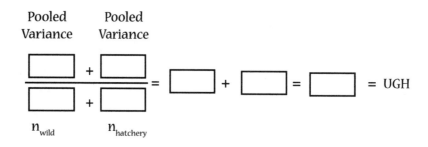

Step 2. Calculate UGH. (This number doesn't have a real name but you will need it in Step 3.)

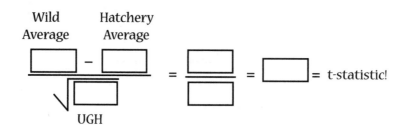

Step 3.

National Science Teachers Association

Corrected Version of Step 2, page 152

Name _____ Page # _____

Practice T-Test Worksheet

(continued)

A couple more things you will need:

Number of Observations of Wild Fish   = [   ] = n_{wild}

Number of Observations of Hatchery Fish   = [   ] = $n_{hatchery}$

Follow the recipe. Think about what information is being incorporated at each step. (You only have to fill in the squares.)

Step 1. Calculate the pooled variance.

$$\frac{\text{Sum of Squares Wild } [\ ] + \text{Sum of Squares Hatchery } [\ ]}{[\ ]\ (n_{wild}-1) + [\ ]\ (n_{hatchery}-1)} = \frac{[\ ]}{[\ ]} = [\ ]\ \text{Pooled Variance}$$

Step 2. Calculate UGH. (This number doesn't have a real name but you will need it in Step 3.)

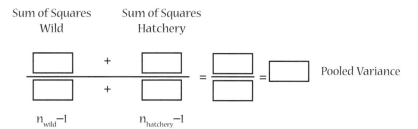

$$\frac{\text{Pooled Variance } [\ ]}{[\ ]\ n_{wild}} + \frac{\text{Pooled Variance } [\ ]}{[\ ]\ n_{hatchery}} = [\ ] + [\ ] = [\ ] = \text{UGH}$$

Step 3.

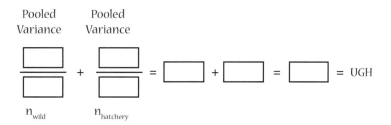

$$\frac{\text{Wild Average } [\ ] - \text{Hatchery Average } [\ ]}{\sqrt{[\ ]\ \text{UGH}}} = \frac{[\ ]}{[\ ]} = [\ ] = \text{t-statistic!}$$

Practice T-Test Worksheet

(continued)

Take a look at the t-table on page 154. You can use it to get a p-value from a t-statistic. Just follow the three steps. (Sometimes it helps to use a ruler and mark the row and column of interest.)

Step 1. Calculate your total number of observations −2. ☐

Step 2. Find the row for your total number of observations −2. = ☐

Step 3. Read across to the number that is closest to your t-statistic but not any bigger. If all the numbers in that row are bigger than your t-statistic, go to step 5. ☐

Step 4. Go up to the top of that column and read off your p-value.

Record your p-value: ☐

Since you stopped at a number that was a little bit smaller than your actual t-statistic, you can say that your p-value is less than that or

$$P < \boxed{}.$$

OK—that means that the odds of the null hypothesis being true are less than ☐.

Step 5. If all the numbers in that row are bigger than your p-value, it means that your p-value is bigger than 0.50. That means that the odds of your null hypothesis being true are greater than ☐.

What do you conclude about your hypothesis? Do you think that your hypothesis is probably true or do you have to keep assuming that your null hypothesis is true?

_____

_____

_____

_____

Practice T-Test Worksheet

(continued)

T-TABLE

p-value Total Observations–2	0.50	0.20	0.10	0.05	0.02	0.01	0.005	0.002	0.001
1	1.00	3.08	6.31	12.71	31.82	63.66	127.32	318.31	636.62
2	0.82	1.89	2.92	4.30	6.97	9.93	14.09	22.33	31.56
3	0.77	1.64	2.35	3.18	4.54	5.84	7.45	10.22	12.92
4	0.74	1.53	2.13	2.78	3.75	4.60	5.60	7.17	8.61
5	0.73	1.48	2.02	2.57	3.37	4.03	4.77	5.89	6.87
6	0.72	1.44	1.94	2.45	3.14	3.71	4.32	5.21	5.96
7	0.71	1.42	1.90	2.37	3.00	3.50	4.03	4.79	5.41
8	0.71	1.40	1.86	2.31	2.90	3.36	3.83	4.50	5.04
9	0.70	1.38	1.83	2.26	2.82	3.25	3.69	4.30	4.78
10	0.70	1.37	1.81	2.23	2.76	3.17	3.58	4.14	4.59
11 - 15	0.70	1.36	1.80	2.20	2.72	3.11	3.50	4.03	4.44
15 - 20	0.70	1.34	1.75	2.13	2.60	2.95	3.29	3.73	4.07
20 - 50	0.69	1.33	1.73	2.09	2.53	2.85	3.15	3.55	4.85
50 - 100	0.68	1.30	1.68	2.01	2.40	2.68	2.94	3.26	3.50

National Science Teachers Association

LTRP: T-Tests

Day 28

Overview

Students now calculate the t-statistic and p-value for their LTRP data. This lesson builds directly on the previous lesson. Students can work in groups, but each student should calculate his or her own statistic. Students can compare results to make sure that they calculated their statistic and p-value correctly.

Focus Question

How does a p-value help you to answer your research question?

Science Skills

- Students should be able to calculate a t-statistic for their LTRP data.

- Students should be able to explain the meaning of a p-value.

- Students should be able to interpret the results of the statistical test in terms of their original research questions.

Background

For background information describing the concepts in this lesson, see "Statistical Testing," page 99; "P-Values," page 101; and "Sampling Variability," page 98.

Materials

- calculators
- T-Test for Real Worksheet (provided)

Development of Lesson

1. The t-test procedures and Worksheet follow the same format as in the previous lesson (Day 27). Depending on the class, it may be necessary to review the steps from the previous lesson. Remind students to work independently so that they can compare results among group members to check for errors. For this calculation, the teacher does not know the answer already so the only way to check for errors will be to compare results within each group.

2. Students may need some assistance at particular steps of their calculations. Suggest to the students that they ask other members of their group or that they refer to the handout from the previous lesson to remind themselves how to use the T-Test for Real Worksheet.

3. Make sure students have time to fill in the answers to the last questions in which they interpret their results.

4. If there is time, meet as a class and have each group share their sample averages, their p-values, and their conclusions. This is a good time to review the fact that different sample averages do not necessarily mean that the null hypothesis isn't true. It's also a good opportunity to coach students in the proper interpretation of their p-values.

Discussion Questions

1. How does your p-value help you to understand your data?

2. Is your p-value surprising or could you predict the answer from your data?

3. If you got a very large p-value, what does it mean?

4. If you had more observations, do you think that you would be more or less likely to have enough evidence to reject your null hypothesis? *With more observations, you would be more likely to have enough evidence to reject your null hypothesis.*

5. If all the observations in each sample were very similar (i.e., you had very little sample variability), how do you think that would affect your p-value? Where in the calculation would this information show up? *If all the observations were very similar, your sum of squares would go down in the first table. As your sum of squares goes down, you would be more likely to have a small enough p-value to reject the null hypothesis. As your sample variability goes down, you are more and more sure that the differences between your treatment averages reflect differences between the population averages.*

Name _____ Page # _____

T-Test For Real Worksheet

Hypothesis:

_____

_____

_____

_____

Null Hypothesis:

_____

_____

_____

_____

The Data

A	B	C	D	E	F	G	H
Treatment 1	Average	Data - Average (A-B)	Difference Squared C^2	Treatment 2	Average	Data - Average (E-F)	Difference Squared G^2
Treatment 1 Average			Total Sum of Squares:	Treatment 2 Average:			Total Sum of Squares:

Name _____ Page # _____

T-Test for Real Worksheet

(continued)

A couple more things you will need:

Number of Observations of Treatment 1 = [ ] = n_1

Number of Observations of Treatment 2 = [ ] = n_2

Follow the recipe. Think about what information is being incorporated at each step. (You will only have to fill in the squares).

Step 1. Calculate the pooled variance.

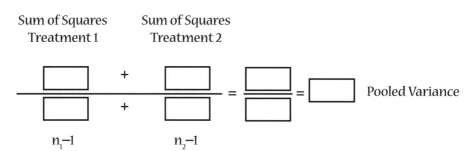

Sum of Squares Treatment 1   Sum of Squares Treatment 2

$$\frac{[\quad] \;+\; [\quad]}{[\quad] \;+\; [\quad]} = \frac{[\quad]}{[\quad]} = [\quad] \quad \text{Pooled Variance}$$

$n_1-1 \qquad\qquad n_2-1$

Step 2. Calculate UGH. (This number doesn't have a real name but you will need it in Step 3.)

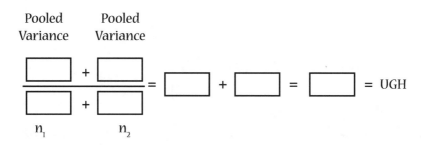

Pooled Variance   Pooled Variance

$$\frac{[\quad] \;+\; [\quad]}{[\quad] \;+\; [\quad]} = [\quad] + [\quad] = [\quad] = \text{UGH}$$

$n_1 \qquad\qquad n_2$

Step 3.

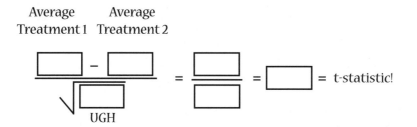

Average Treatment 1   Average Treatment 2

$$\frac{[\quad] \;-\; [\quad]}{\sqrt{[\quad]}} = \frac{[\quad]}{[\quad]} = [\quad] = \text{t-statistic!}$$

UGH

158

National Science Teachers Association

Corrected Version of Step 2, page 158

Name _____ Page # _____

T-Test for Real Worksheet

(continued)

A couple more things you will need:

Number of Observations of Treatment 1 $\quad = \boxed{} = n_1$

Number of Observations of Treatment 2 $\quad = \boxed{} = n_2$

Follow the recipe. Think about what information is being incorporated at each step. (You will only have to fill in the squares).

Step 1. Calculate the pooled variance.

Sum of Squares Treatment 1   Sum of Squares Treatment 2

$$\frac{\boxed{} \;+\; \boxed{}}{\underset{n_1-1}{\boxed{}} \;+\; \underset{n_2-1}{\boxed{}}} = \frac{\boxed{}}{\boxed{}} = \boxed{} \quad \text{Pooled Variance}$$

Step 2. Calculate UGH. (This number doesn't have a real name but you will need it in Step 3.)

Pooled Variance   Pooled Variance

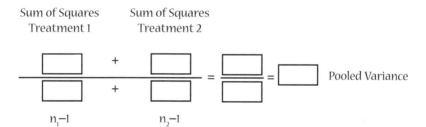

$$\frac{\boxed{}}{\underset{n_1}{\boxed{}}} \;+\; \frac{\boxed{}}{\underset{n_2}{\boxed{}}} = \boxed{} + \boxed{} = \boxed{} = \text{UGH}$$

Step 3.

Average Treatment 1   Average Treatment 2

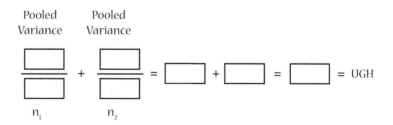

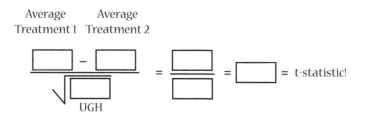

$$\frac{\boxed{} - \boxed{}}{\sqrt{}} = \frac{\boxed{}}{\boxed{}} = \boxed{} = \text{t-statistic!}$$

UGH

National Science Teachers Association

T-Test for Real Worksheet

(continued)

Yea! Now you have your t-statistic. Record the absolute value of your t-statistic in the double box!

Step 1. Calculate your total number of observations −2. ☐

Step 2. Find the row for your total number of observations −2. = ☐

Step 3. Read across to the number that is closest to your t-statistic but not any bigger. If all the numbers in that row are bigger than your t-statistic, go to step 5. ☐

Step 4. Go up to the top of that column and read off your p-value.

Record your p-value: ☐

Since you stopped at a number that was a little bit smaller than your actual t-statistic, you can say that your p-value is less than that or

P < ☐ .

OK—that means that the odds of the null hypothesis being true are less than ☐ .

Step 5. If all the numbers in that row are bigger than your p-value, it means that your p-value is bigger than 0.50. That means that the odds of your null hypothesis being true are greater than ☐ .

Would you say that you can reject the null hypothesis or would you say that you cannot reject the null hypothesis based on your p-value?

_____

_____

_____

Based on your knowledge of the subject, the field site, and your data, would you say that this is a valid conclusion? Why or why not?

_____

_____

_____

T-Test for Real Worksheet

(continued)

T-TABLE

p-value / Total Observations−2	0.50	0.20	0.10	0.05	0.02	0.01	0.005	0.002	0.001
1	1.00	3.08	6.31	12.71	31.82	63.66	127.32	318.31	636.62
2	0.82	1.89	2.92	4.30	6.97	9.93	14.09	22.33	31.56
3	0.77	1.64	2.35	3.18	4.54	5.84	7.45	10.22	12.92
4	0.74	1.53	2.13	2.78	3.75	4.60	5.60	7.17	8.61
5	0.73	1.48	2.02	2.57	3.37	4.03	4.77	5.89	6.87
6	0.72	1.44	1.94	2.45	3.14	3.71	4.32	5.21	5.96
7	0.71	1.42	1.90	2.37	3.00	3.50	4.03	4.79	5.41
8	0.71	1.40	1.86	2.31	2.90	3.36	3.83	4.50	5.04
9	0.70	1.38	1.83	2.26	2.82	3.25	3.69	4.30	4.78
10	0.70	1.37	1.81	2.23	2.76	3.17	3.58	4.14	4.59
11 - 15	0.70	1.36	1.80	2.20	2.72	3.11	3.50	4.03	4.44
15 - 20	0.70	1.34	1.75	2.13	2.60	2.95	3.29	3.73	4.07
20 - 50	0.69	1.33	1.73	2.09	2.53	2.85	3.15	3.55	4.85
50 - 100	0.68	1.30	1.68	2.01	2.40	2.68	2.94	3.26	3.50

LTRP: RESULTS PARAGRAPH

Day 29

Overview

Students work together to write the results paragraph for their poster presentations. The results paragraph should explain in detail exactly what patterns appear in the data. The results paragraph does not discuss the meaning of the data; it summarizes the patterns. This section includes the results paragraph, a table of the data, and graphs of the data. The results paragraph should describe the information in the table and graphs with text. It may also contain observations about unusual data points, variability between observations, or uncontrolled factors. More details on the results versus the discussion section are provided in the overview for LTRP: Discussion Paragraph (Days 31, 32). An assessment rubric is included at the end of the lesson.

Focus Question

How can you describe research results in words?

Science Skills

■ Students should be able to describe and summarize data presented in a table.

■ Students should be able to describe and summarize data presented in a graph.

■ Students should be able to differentiate between reporting the data patterns and interpreting the data patterns.

Background

For background information describing the concepts in this lesson, see "Four Parts of a Scientific Report," page 2.

Materials

■ Writing Results Worksheet (provided)

■ handout: Example Results Paragraphs (provided)

The Worksheet is easier to use if copied onto two pages rather than one double-sided page. If students did not complete the two t-test lessons, they should use the p-value that they estimated from the Stat Savvy lesson (Day 26).

Development of Lesson

1. As a class, discuss the difference between the results paragraph and the discussion

paragraph (to be written on Days 31, 32). The results paragraph describes the data and the discussion paragraph interprets the data. The handout, Example Results Paragraphs, can be discussed by the class. What is confusing about the different examples? What is good? Would it have helped to have the units described for each number?

2. Useful information and ideas for the results paragraph were generated during the graphing lessons (Days 23, 24) and the Stat Savvy lesson (Day 26). Remind students of the graphical analysis questions from that lesson.

- What patterns appear in the graphs?

- Do the graphs appear to support or reject the null hypothesis?

- Given the amount of variability in the data, is the graph of the two averages a very good description of the data?

- Are there any unusual data points?

- Do the unusual data points have a very big effect on the average value for the treatment?

- Would the patterns still look the same without these unusual data points?

- Can the students remember anything about measuring that replicate in the field that might explain why it is so large or so small (refer students to their Data Collection Notes Worksheet [Day 21])?

- Looking at the two graphs of the raw data, does it seem as if there were any uncontrolled factors that influenced the data?

3. Review the Writing Results Worksheet with the class. Students should use the example sentences as models, particularly for describing the p-value.

4. Have students work together in their LTRP groups to draft the results paragraph for their poster presentations. They will need to have copies of their graphs, data tables, and statistical analysis results readily available. Each member of the group should have a copy of the paragraph on his or her worksheet.

5. If necessary, review strategies for writing cooperatively. Encourage students to outline the paragraph first. What sentences need to be included? Group members can decide to write independent paragraphs and combine them at the end of the class.

Discussion Questions

1. What patterns do you see in your graph?

2. Can you see the same patterns in the table?

3. Are there specific replicates (cells in your table) that should be pointed out to the reader—for example, surprisingly large or small observations that may have a big effect on the average?

4. Does the information from your graph match the information from your p-value?

5. What does the p-value mean exactly?

6. What is the difference between describing and interpreting the data?

Writing Results Worksheet

Look at your data table, your graph, and the results of your statistical analysis or evaluation (p-value). Discuss the patterns in your data with your group. What are the major patterns in the data table and the graph? Which treatment seems to have bigger or smaller observations or do they look the same? Does any one replicate observation seem to have a strong influence on the average? Can you see differences between the data collected on different days? Make a note of these differences so you don't forget.

_____

_____

_____

_____

_____

What does your p-value tell you? The last sentences of your results paragraph should state the p-value and explain exactly what it means for your data. You can base your sentences on the following example sentences:

"We did/estimated a t-test on our data and calculated/estimated a p-value of 0.04. Our p-value means that there is only a 4 percent chance of getting these data if the null hypothesis is true. We reject the null hypothesis. We conclude that our hypothesis is probably true and that there are different amounts of rain in the field and in the forest."

OR

"We did/estimated a t-test on our data and calculated/estimated a p-value of 0.32. Our p-value means that there is a 32 percent chance of getting these data if our null hypothesis is true. There is not enough evidence to say that our null hypothesis probably isn't true so we cannot reject the null hypothesis. We continue to assume that the amount of rain is the same in the field versus the forest."

REMEMBER: You can't prove the null hypothesis is true; you can only say, "We continue to assume that the null hypothesis is true" or "We did not reject the null hypothesis."

Imagine that you are giving someone a guided tour of your table and graphs. Using your graphs, data tables, notes, and the example sentences, write your results paragraph on the following lines or on a piece of lined paper. You should have one sentence for each point you want to make.

_____

_____

_____

_____

_____

_____

_____

_____

_____

_____

_____

_____

_____

_____

_____

_____

_____

_____

_____

_____

_____

_____

_____

_____

Reread the paragraph out loud. Do all the sentences flow together? If you have extra time, type the paragraph onto your disk. Remember to save it as a new file with a new name or add it to the end of one of your other paragraphs. Have at least one person who didn't do the typing spell-check and proofread carefully.

Example Results Paragraphs

Example 1

We found a range of 0–25 insects in one sample. The average of the number of bugs found under the top bridge and under the bottom bridge are different by 0.4. The top bridge has one high number that affects the data. The number is 24. Without this number, the average is 5.3 instead of 7.3. The bottom has two high numbers, 20 and 25. Without these, the average is 4.3 and it was originally 6.9. Without the extreme numbers, the averages are farther apart—1.0 instead of 4.0—but the number of bugs found under the top bridge is still higher. All the high data points for both bridges were found on the second day. We didn't find as many bugs on the first day. The odds of getting these data if the null hypothesis is true is 50 percent. That is our p-value.

Example 2

Our average for airplane flight distance near the buildings is 7.92 meters, whereas the average flight distance on top of the hill was 13.5 meters. The difference between the averages is 5.58. The data from the building sites were much more variable than the data from the hill sites. Most observations by the building were between 10 and 15 m. There are no influential data points. All the numbers were close and ranged from 2–15. The odds of getting these data if the null hypothesis is true is 0.1 percent. We reject the null hypothesis and conclude that there is a difference in airplane flight distances near the building versus on top of the hill.

Example 3

The average temperature of the lake at the stream's entrance is 9.17°C and the average temperature farther out towards the middle of the lake is 10.69°C. The reason that the average toward the middle of the lake is higher is that one replicate was taken farther out than the others by a kayaker and the rest were only as far as we could throw. That one replicate greatly influenced our average. Without this replicate, the average of the lake is 10.36°C. The p-value is 0.01. We used the average of 10.69 in finding our p-value. That means that the odds of getting these data if the null hypothesis is true is 1 percent. Our null hypothesis stated that there is no difference in temperature between the lake at stream's entrance and farther out in the lake. We conclude that there is a difference.

ASSESSMENT RUBRIC

LTRP: Results Paragraph (Day 29)

	Beginner	Intermediate	Proficient	Advanced
Tables and Graphs	Presents information that does not match data tables and graphs. Does not demonstrate an understanding of graphical results.	Presents information that matches data tables and graphs.	Presents information that matches data tables and graphs and includes averages and p-values.	Accurate and detailed description of tables and graphs and includes averages, ranges, evaluation of unusual data points, and p-values.
Interpretation	Includes some interpretation of results.	Includes some interpretation of results.	Does not interpret results.	Does not interpret results.
T-Tests	Does not state t-test results correctly.	Does not state t-test results correctly.	States t-test results correctly and uses model sentences on worksheet.	States t-test results correctly and uses own words to present results.
Null Hypothesis	Does not state whether or not the null hypothesis can be rejected.	Does not state whether or not the null hypothesis can be rejected.	States whether or not the null hypothesis can be rejected.	States clearly whether or not the null hypothesis can be rejected.

LTRP: Library Research II

Day 30

Overview

The purpose of the second library visit is to find answers to the question "How can we explain our experimental results?" This task requires the students to use critical reasoning skills to determine the validity of their results given the information available. For example, a group may find more mushrooms in the forest than an open field. In the group members' discussion paragraph (Days 31and 32), they must use evidence from their research and from background information to explain why they got this result. In the library they can read about fungi and mushrooms, how they grow, where they grow, necessary environmental conditions, plant associations, etc. This information provides a broader understanding of the research question and gives the results context. Because each experiment is different, each library quest will be different.

Focus Question

What is already known about our research question that can help us explain our results?

Science Skills

- Students should be able to find information in books, CD-ROMs, or webpages that contain relevant information to help explain research results.

- Students should be able to take notes from the source and identify information that helps explain research results.

- Students should be able to keep a standard bibliography of relevant sources.

Background

For background information describing the concepts in this lesson, see "Four Parts of a Scientific Report," page 2, and "Library Research I," page 43.

Materials

- Library Research I Worksheet (Day 9) (provided, page 46)
- Library Research II Worksheet (provided)
- library access
- Internet access (optional)

Development of Lesson

1. Begin the lesson with a class discussion of the research results. The groups may not be aware of what other groups discovered. Have each group state its research question and summarize the results. Encourage students to ask questions of each other. This will help them clarify their own understanding of the project.

2. Continue the class discussion, asking the groups why they think they got the results they did. What do they know about the system or topic that helps explain the results? What information could they try to find that could help them explain the results?

3. Tell the students they now have an opportunity to use the library to try to find more information to help explain their results. Encourage the group members to work individually or in pairs to maximize the amount of library research completed. Use the Library Research II Worksheet to structure the library work if necessary. Remind students to keep track of their sources and to use the standard bibliography format given on the Library Research I Worksheet.

4. If students feel they have exhausted all possible sources in the library, encourage them to use the Internet and school science textbooks. The librarian may be able to suggest alternative sources.

Discussion Questions

1. Describe your research question and results. Why do you think you got these results?

2. What type of information could help you explain the results better?

3. How could you find this information?

4. What questions might someone else (who didn't do the research) ask you about your results?

5. How might your experimental design (methods) have influenced or affected your results?

6. What additional research questions could you ask based on your results?

Library Research II Worksheet

1. Which hypothesis do your data support? (circle one)

Null hypothesis   OR   Hypothesis

What did you discover by doing your research and analyzing the results?

_____

_____

_____

2. Go back to your notes from your first visit to the library. What background information helps support your results? What background information seems to disagree with your results? You may need to look again at some of your original sources or look for new sources.

Evidence from background information or new sources that is consistent with our results:

Source: _____

Evidence: _____

_____

_____

_____

_____

_____

Evidence from background information or new sources that is inconsistent with our results:

Source: _____

Evidence: _____

_____

_____

_____

_____

_____

Describe any additional evidence that is consistent or inconsistent with your results on an additional sheet of paper.

Days 31, 32

Overview

Students work in their research groups to write one paragraph or more that interprets their results and provides a conclusion for the overall project. This is not a concrete task, and the students may need encouragement to think critically about their overall experiment and the results. The results must be placed in context using topical information from the library research and a general understanding of experimental design. Why did we get these results? What do they mean? What have we learned about the system? Is there any way our experimental design may have biased our results? The paragraph is scripted in the Discussion Paragraph Workshop so that all groups will be able to complete the task. Groups that would like to elaborate should be encouraged to do so. On the second day of this lesson, students have time to type their results and discussion paragraphs into the computer.

Focus Question

How do scientists write conclusions to their research reports?

Science Skills

■ Students should be able to synthesize information from their experimental design, results, and library research.

■ Students should be able to write a concluding paragraph that interprets experimental results based on general information about the topic and the methods employed.

Background

For background information describing the concepts in this lesson, see "Four Parts of a Scientific Report," page 2.

Materials

■ Discussion Paragraph Worksheet (provided)

■ access to computer lab

Development of Lesson

1. Ask the students to describe differences between the results and discussion sections of a research report. What type of information is included in the discussion? Review the questions from part 3 on the Discussion Paragraph Worksheet.

2. Hand out the worksheets and go over the example discussion paragraphs on the back. These paragraphs were written by students. What do your students like about the paragraphs? How could they be improved?

3. Review the Discussion Paragraph Worksheet with the class. Remind students to use information from their Data Collection Notes (Day 21), Results Paragraph (Day 29) and Library Research I and II (Days 9, 30).

4. Have students work together in LTRP groups to write the final paragraph for their research reports. Each group must cooperatively write at least one discussion paragraph as they did when they wrote the results. Everyone should have a copy of the paragraph.

5. If necessary, review with students strategies for writing a paragraph together. Select one person to write sentences for the group. Follow the directions on the Discussion Paragraph Worksheet. Each person suggests an idea for each sentence. The group discusses the different ideas and crafts a new sentence using the strong parts of each suggested sentence. The final sentence is recorded, reread, and agreed on by all. If a group has a hard time working together, each student can write a discussion paragraph. The group will review the paragraphs together and choose the best one for the final project. Or, they may be able to take parts of each paragraph to draft the final one.

6. By the end of the second day, all the groups should have their results and discussion paragraphs typed into the computer. It will help the teacher to prepare for the next lesson if all the groups turn in one copy of each of the LTRP paragraphs: introduction, methods, results, and discussion. If student groups are behind in producing and typing paragraphs, take time to finish them now.

Discussion Questions

1. Why do you think your results turned out the way they did?

2. Is there any way your methods might have influenced the results? Explain why or why not.

3. What type of information could help you explain the results better?

4. How do your results compare with your original prediction? Did this surprise you? Why or why not?

5. What additional research questions could you ask based on your results?

6. What have you learned about your research topic that you didn't know when you started the project?

Discussion Paragraph Worksheet

The discussion paragraph is similar to a conclusion. In this paragraph, you discuss how your research helps us understand something new about the topic. What has your research taught you that you didn't know when you started the project?

1. Start your paragraph with a sentence summarizing the results.

"Our research showed that (*there is no difference in the number of stream invertebrates found in upstream and downstream sections of the St. Edward Park stream).*"

2. The second sentence should state which hypothesis your research supports.

"The results (*do/do not*) support our original hypothesis."

3. Now continue writing your discussion using the following questions as a guide. Look at your data collection notes and library research notes for ideas.

- ■ Why do you think there is or is not a difference?

- ■ Do your results make sense given what you already know about the topic? Remember you can't claim that your results are true everywhere unless you collected data everywhere.

- ■ How might the methods you used affect or bias your results?

- ■ Did your results surprise you in any way? If so, how?

- ■ If you were to do the research again, what changes would you make and why?

_____
_____
_____
_____
_____
_____
_____
_____
_____
_____

Reread the paragraph to make sure that someone who didn't do the research can understand what you are explaining. Make any necessary changes. Everyone in the group must agree with the final paragraph. Choose group members to type this paragraph and the results paragraph onto your project disk. Save each file by a new name (such as, "Discussion" and "Results"). Then, spell-check, proofread, and print one copy of each paragraph.

Example Discussion Paragraphs

1. Research Question: Is there more sediment in a stagnant pond or a fast-moving creek?

DISCUSSION:

Our investigation showed that there is more sediment in a stagnant pond than in a fast-moving creek. This supported our hypothesis that there will be more sediment in the pond than in the creek. The t-test ($p < 0.10$) showed that there is a 10 percent chance that our test would support our null hypothesis. So, for every 100 tests, 10 of them would show no difference in the sediment load if the null hypothesis were true. If we were to do it again, we would use bigger nets.

2. Research Question: Do more macroscopic invertebrates live in stream or pond muck?

DISCUSSION:

There were many more invertebrates in the pond muck than there were in the stream muck (statistically significant). We think the reason that that's true is because the stream muck is just sand, whereas the pond's muck is very rich with nutrients and there's lots of other life for them to live on, with, and in. The lower the water was, the more macroscopic invertebrates we found in the pond. We think that we found more invertebrates when the water was shallower because maybe they like thicker muck and the muck is thick without as much water.

3. Research Question: Does a potato make more electricity than a turnip?

DISCUSSION:

Our hypothesis was that there would be more electricity from a potato than a turnip. According to our averages, potatoes do make more electricity than turnips. Our t-test shows no statistical difference between the amount of electricity made by the two kinds of tuber, which supports our null hypothesis. We had fun doing this experiment and if you tried it too, you would have as much fun as we did, because this experiment is repeatable.

ASSESSMENT RUBRIC

Discussion Paragraph (Days 31, 32)

	Beginner	Intermediate	Proficient	Advanced
Presentation of Results	Restates results without relating them to research question and background information.	Restates results and offers personal ideas of why they got these results.	Restates results and presents conclusions that relate to research question and background information.	Presents a clear and concise interpretation of how results relate to research question and to background information.
Discussion of Possible Bias	Does not discuss how methods may have biased results.	Does not discuss how methods may have biased results.	Discusses how methods may have biased results.	Discusses how methods may have biased results and suggests alternative methods.
Suggestions for Improvement	Does not suggest ways to improve the experiment.	Suggests very few changes to research project or changes that are inconsequential.	Suggests relevant changes that could improve research project.	Suggests relevant changes and other experiments to improve understanding of system.

PRESENTATION OF RESEARCH PROJECTS

Background Information

In this final section of the curriculum, Long-Term Research Project (LTRP) groups prepare poster and oral presentations of their projects. The momentum builds to the final celebration when parents, teachers, and other students are invited to view the posters and listen to the presentations. Arrangements for a suitable space for the presentations should have already been made. Invitations/reminders can be sent to parents. To prepare for the presentations, the students will review and give suggestions to improve each other's projects (Day 33) just as scientists do before publishing research results. Three days are devoted to making the posters (Days 34, 35, 36) and three days are devoted to preparing oral presentations (Days 37, 38, 39). Finally, the students practice their presentations within their groups and then for the class (Day 40). The big show is the grand finale of the curriculum. Having the project culminate in a final presentation with an audience really drives students to produce high-quality products. Be prepared for high anxiety levels, especially if students have not had much experience on stage. They do fine if they have practiced, and they generally feel great about themselves and their accomplishments once they complete the presentations.

Peer Review Process

Scientific journals (e.g., *Science, Nature, Ecology, Journal of the American Medical Association* [*JAMA*]) differ from science magazines (e.g., *Discover, Popular Science, Scientific American*) in several ways. In scientific journals, scientists write the articles and anonymous reviewers, considered to be experts in the area of research, critique the articles. For an article or paper to be published, reviewers must recommend the article; most articles are rejected the first time they are reviewed. The author receives all the suggestions and criticisms from the reviewers, takes a deep breath, and rewrites and resubmits the article. This process helps to ensure that articles published in scientific journals meet a high standard. Reviewers verify that the research is presented accurately and that the statistical analyses and interpretations of results are justified. In science magazines, on the other hand, journalists usually write the articles. Editors for the journal or magazine review all of the articles and decide which ones will be published and what changes should be made. Science magazines also have lots of advertising, which scientific journals usually avoid.

Students can learn a lot by going through the process of scientific review as if their reports were to be published in a scientific journal. They have focused on their own project for so long, it is helpful to step back and look at what a different group has done, give feedback, and get feedback from a new audience. The process reinforces the idea of producing a rough draft that is reviewed before completing the finished paper.

Poster Presentations

Poster presentations are a standard way for scientists to present research results at conferences. Usually a room is set aside where posters are mounted on walls or stand on tables. During a poster session, the public can view the posters while the researchers are present to answer questions. It is very interesting to walk through a room full of science posters and be able to talk informally with the people who did the research. The poster presentation in this project does not emphasize this kind of interaction, but it can be adapted to include a session where other students in the school or in other science classes can view the posters and ask questions of the researchers.

Keep your eyes open for any science research poster contests that students could enter. Several groups to check for such contests are the American Statistical Association, the National Science Teachers Association, and Westinghouse Science Research Competitions. They all have webpages that include information on poster contests. You could also arrange a poster contest within the school. Select a panel of teachers, local scientists, school board members, and other interested people from the extended school community to serve as judges. Names must not be visible on the posters for the judging to be valid. The parent group or a local merchant may be able to donate a prize for the winning poster.

Oral Presentations

Giving oral presentations of research projects is a standard way of communicating research results at scientific conferences, university seminars, and academic job interviews. The length of the presentation varies from 15 to 50 minutes depending on the situation. (For student projects, we recommend five-minute presentations.) Many disciplines rely on computer-generated slide presentations while others use overhead transparencies. Occasionally video clips are included if they improve the audience's understanding of the research. At the end of the presentation, the speaker is expected to respond to questions from the audience. Although this can be a nerve-racking aspect of giving an oral presentation, it helps the scientist examine the results from different perspectives.

In this curriculum unit, the final celebration includes a poster display and a three- to five-minute oral presentation from each LTRP group. Inviting parents and including food and beverages adds to the celebratory atmosphere. This celebration is similar to the performance of a play that students have studied and rehearsed for several months. It is the big night, a wonderful opportunity to get parents and administrators involved and a chance to show off the accomplishments of some young scientists. Have fun with this and congratulate yourself for training a new group of scientific thinkers!

LTRP: Peer Reviews

Day 33

Overview

The goal of this lesson is to help students think critically about their research reports and to demonstrate how standards in scientific research are maintained. The lesson presents some logistical difficulties in that it requires all groups to have typed and printed all four paragraphs of their research report (introduction, methods, results, discussion). The teacher makes enough photocopies of the reports so that each person in the class can proofread and critique a different group's report. These should be anonymous reviews, so writers' names are blocked out and reviewers do not place their name on the paper. Reviewers are instructed to look for grammatical errors and overall clarity. Encourage students to point out parts that they like or that are well written and to make suggestions to improve other parts. An assessment rubric is included at the end of this lesson.

Focus Question

How do scientists maintain a high standard for research?

Science Skills

- Students should be able to proofread an anonymous report for errors having to do with spelling, punctuation, subject-verb agreement, etc.

- Students should be able to recognize parts in an anonymous report that are written clearly, concisely, and thoroughly.

- Students should be able to make constructive suggestions to improve an anonymous report.

- Students should be able to assess the validity of the comments of anonymous reviewers and use them to improve the research report.

Background

For background information describing the concepts in this lesson, see "Four Parts of a Scientific Report," page 2, and "Peer Review Process," page 175.

Materials

- copies of every group's research reports (introduction, methods, results, discussion—without names)

- Peer Reviews Worksheet (provided)

Development of Lesson

1. Before class, make photocopies of each LTRP group's research report (introduction, methods, results, and discussion). You will need enough copies so each student can review one research report from a different group. Be sure the names of group members have been removed or blacked out so the reviews can be anonymous. If some groups do not have their paragraphs ready, you may omit theirs from being reviewed. Be sure these groups review someone else's report, even if their own won't be reviewed.

2. Show the class a copy of a scientific or education journal, if available. Explain to the class that all the reports in the journal are read by the editor and several other scientists before they are published. Ask the class why this is done. There are many reasons the students can give. Focus the discussion on the desire to maintain a high standard (reports are accurate, well written, follow a certain format, contain studies with strong experimental designs, etc.) and the value of feedback in maintaining that standard. When a poor-quality research report is included in a journal, it embarrasses editors, reviewers, and other scientists who have contributed to the journal.

3. Inform the students that today they will review research reports written by other groups. Discuss the kinds of comments that are helpful to writers. Encourage them to make constructive suggestions and to focus on how they can help each other improve the final product. For example, a constructive comment does not simply point out that something is wrong or unclear; it suggests how it could be changed. Remind students that insults do not help and are not acceptable comments.

4. Instruct students to first read the report and correct any mechanical errors (such as spelling and punctuation). Read the report a second time and mark sections that are good (complete, thorough, well-written, easy to understand). Read the report a third time and make suggestions to improve parts that are weak (difficult to understand, parts have been left out, vague, too many unclear pronouns, confusing).

5. After completing the reviews, collect the papers and quickly scan them for inappropriate comments.

6. Return reviews to the research groups. Have research groups read all comments and decide which ones to change and which ones to ignore. Some comments may reflect a misunderstanding of factual information and can be ignored. Often, comments that authors view as "wrong" indicate a need to clarify a point in the report. Some suggestions may be impractical or off base.

7. Rewrite and retype the reports based on the comments received.

   Note: The reviews generally do not take much time, maybe 15 minutes. That leaves enough time to rewrite and retype any needed changes. A few groups might need more time.

Discussion Questions

1. Why do scientists always have research reports reviewed by other scientists before they are published?

2. What kind of comments help you write better?

3. State some positive ways of criticizing someone else's writing.

4. How do you feel when you read comments and criticisms of your work?

5. How can you decide which comments to include as you rewrite your report?

6. What other work that you do in school would benefit from being reviewed by someone else?

7. How many drafts does it take to write a good paper? Why?

Peer Reviews Worksheet

When scientists write about their experiments, other scientists usually read, proofread, and make suggestions about the paper. This is what you will do today for the fellow scientists in your class. Remember, you are reading these paragraphs to help someone else, so be sure to make your suggestions constructive.

Follow these directions:

1. Read the report through once. Underline any words that you think are misspelled and correct any mechanical mistakes (e.g., missing words, punctuation, capital letters, sentences that are too long, incomplete sentences).

2. Read the report a second time. Mark sections that are good and don't need to be changed (easy to understand and contain all necessary information).

3. Read the report a third time. Suggest changes in parts that are unclear or difficult to understand and need to be rewritten.

4. Read each of the following statements and rate the report you read on a scale from 1 to 3: 1—needs improvement; 2—good; 3—excellent.

_____   Introduction provides a clear background for the project.

_____   Research question is clearly stated.

_____   Methods are complete and thorough.

_____   The experiment could be repeated following the methods.

_____   Results summarize data.

_____   Results section presents the probability of getting the data if the null hypothesis is true.

_____   Discussion tries to explain results.

_____   Discussion describes the group's reaction to the results. (The results surprised/did not surprise us.)

_____   The ideas are clearly expressed.

5. Are there any specific and helpful suggestions you could make to this group to improve the quality of their report?

_____

_____

_____

_____

ASSESSMENT RUBRIC

Peer Reviews (Day 33)

	Beginner	Intermediate	Proficient	Advanced
Proofreading	Has difficulty proofreading and identifying grammatical errors.	Proofreads and identifies most grammatical errors.	Proofreads effectively for grammatical errors.	Proofreads effectively for grammatical errors.
Identifying Strong Aspects of Reports	Makes only general and limited statements about paragraphs.	Points out at least one part that is written clearly, concisely, and thoroughly.	Points out parts of report that are written clearly, concisely, and thoroughly.	Points out parts of report that are written clearly, concisely, and thoroughly.
Making Suggestions	Reading other reports does not help student improve own report.	Makes at least one constructive suggestion.	Makes constructive suggestions to improve report.	Makes insightful and constructive suggestions to improve report.
Using the Peer Review Process	Unable to make corrections based on reviews by others.	Able to make corrections based on reviews by others and from experience reviewing other projects.	Able to make corrections based on reviews by others and from experience reviewing other projects.	Has a much better understanding of how to improve own report after having evaluated other reports.

The Truth about Science

Days 34, 35, 36

LTRP: POSTER PREPARATION

Overview

Students prepare and polish their posters during these three periods. The teacher's role during this time is to keep the students focused and on task. If the class is planning to submit the posters to a local or national contest, the teacher should check beforehand to make sure that the posters will meet all the requirements of the competition (e.g., size, location of student names, format).

Focus Question
N/A

Science Skills
- Students should be able to work in groups to produce a final product.
- Students should be able to organize their time to complete a large project.

Background
For background information describing the concepts in this lesson, see Appendix B: Example Posters; "Poster Presentations," page 176; and "Four Parts of a Scientific Report," page 2.

Materials
- 1 poster board per group (color requests may be possible if orders are taken in advance)
- blank paper, graph paper, colored paper
- markers, pens, pencils
- scissors, paper cutter, ruler, glue sticks
- pictures from field trips, if available
- field samples (small branches, fern fronds, etc.) for decorating posters (The field samples should be pressed or covered with clear contact paper.)

Development of Lesson

1. Discuss as a group what should be included in a poster presentation. A photograph of a sample poster about the worm experiments and photographs of student posters are provided in Appendix B: Example Posters. These can be used as examples. The four elements of a research report should all be presented in order: introduction, methods, results, discussion. Students should also put at least one bibliographic reference on the poster. Students may want to include a list of materials, a site map, photographs of their research, examples of a data sheet, pressed leaves or other specimens, magazine pictures, and drawings or photographs from the Web. Ideas about what to include are presented in "Four Parts of a Scientific Report," page 2.

   Note: Students may each create a poster instead of working on one group poster. Individual posters will take longer but students may stay more focused. Evaluations can be based on individual rather than group work.

2. Have each LTRP group draw a poster plan on a blank sheet of paper. Their plan should include the poster title, a list of elements to be included, and a sketch of where each element will go.

3. After the teacher has approved the plan, students can begin working. Some groups may need to spend time typing and or editing their paragraphs at the computer. Other groups may want to make new hand-drawn or computer graphs. Students should read Appendix D, especially "Tips on Saving Documents" if they are using the computer. All posters need a title and headings. Students need to be encouraged to have all group members working if they want to complete their poster in time (rather than two students observing and commenting as a third draws the title).

4. At the end of each class, have the students put all their group materials into one place—an envelope or a file—so nothing gets lost or damaged between work periods.

5. Before gluing or writing on the poster board, students should make one final check by laying all the pieces on the board. Check that all four parts of a research report are included, that appropriate references are listed, that graphs are well labeled, that legends are present where needed, and that the paragraphs are free of glaring typos. You may want to require each group to get teacher approval of its poster layout before gluing begins. You may also want to photocopy graphs and artwork before gluing so they can be used for the oral presentation.

6. Students can now glue the poster together. Store posters somewhere very safe after they have been completed.

Discussion Questions

1. What elements make a poster exciting? Fun to look at? Easy to read?

2. What was the most difficult part of preparing the poster?

3. Is there anything you could have done earlier in the project that would have helped with preparing your poster?

4. How is preparing a poster different from writing a report?

Days 37, 38, 39 — LTRP: PREPARING RESEARCH PRESENTATIONS

Overview

During these three days, students create visual aids to use during their oral scientific presentations. At the beginning of the lesson, students view an overhead presentation (Appendix C: Worm Presentation) on data from Wigglin' Worms (Days 13, 14) and discuss the differences between written and oral presentations. The presentation can be used to demonstrate presentation styles, incorporation of background Materials, and/or formatting of visual aids. Students use the rest of the class time to outline their group presentations and prepare overhead transparencies to guide the audience. This process pushes students to review their experiences and to determine the most important points of their research projects. They must summarize these experiences and ideas with only a few written words on the visual aids. Students can use lots of words to explain an idea when they speak, but the words on the visual aids should be simple. Visual aids can also include maps, graphs, and drawings—some can be copied from the poster and others will need to be drawn for the first time.

Focus Questions

How do you prepare clear and simple visual aids for oral presentations? What kind of language is best for explaining scientific research orally?

Science Skills

- Students should be able to outline their entire research process.
- Students should be able to state the most important aspects of their research.
- Students should be able to create clear visual aids.
- Students should be able to script a clear and concise scientific presentation.

Background

For background information describing the concepts in this lesson, see "Four Parts of a Scientific Presentation," page 2, and "Oral Presentations," page 176.

Materials

- overhead transparencies (about 8 per research group)
- permanent markers
- index cards
- access to a copy machine
- Appendix C: Worm Presentation copied onto transparencies
- Preparing Your Presentation Worksheet (provided)
- Practicing Your Presentation Worksheet (provided)

Development of Lesson

1. Start by discussing the celebration. All the students should already know that the celebration is coming but they may not have thought about their own presentations yet.

2. Give the example presentation on worm data (Appendix C) to the class. Afterward, discuss the difference between a poster presentation and an oral presentation. How many words were on each transparency? How large were the words? How was the presentation organized? What was fun about it? What was boring?

3. Read the Preparing Your Presentation Worksheet together as a class. Solicit suggestions for interesting things to include on the visual aids for each section. For example, students who studied bugs could include pictures or sketches of the main bugs they found. Remind the students that they are not starting from scratch again; all the ideas that they need are in their science notebooks. Is there information from the data collection notes that they would like to include in the methods or the discussion section? Are there interesting facts from their first library research trip that might make the introduction more exciting?

4. Remind students that they only have room for "word clues" on their overhead transparencies. Word clues are just a few words that remind the speaker what he or she needs to say and that help the audience follow along. For example, the introduction overheads do not need to contain full sentences but rather a bullet list of one- or two-word phrases that help the audience follow what is being said. As students create these overheads, they can write down what they will actually say on index cards.

5. Review the difference between written and oral language. A reader can go back and reread a confusing sentence but a listener cannot go back and replay it. Oral sentences must be simpler and shorter than written sentences. All scientific words need to be defined.

6. For the remainder of the class, students work in their LTRP groups to create a series of overheads and a script for their presentation. The first step is to decide who will be in charge of each section and to identify a list of all the overheads that need to be created.

7. When the teacher has approved the presentation organization, students can begin working on their overheads. They can use the Preparing Your Presentation Worksheet as a guide, checking off each box as they complete that item. Some groups will need only four overheads: others will require many. It works best if students draft the overheads on blank paper. The teacher can check for font size and clarity before students begin working on the actual transparencies. The drafts can easily be traced onto the transparencies. When students are writing directly on the overhead transparencies, it may be best to use permanent markers so that the overheads don't smudge as they are handled or as details are added. Some groups may want to trace items from their posters. Groups may also print out words and graphs from the computer for the teacher to photocopy onto overheads. Students should not use whole paragraphs or even long sentences from their poster but rather bulleted lists. The lists can be printed in a large font, but the teacher may have to further enlarge the text when copying.

8. As students work on their visual aids, they can write down what they will be saying during the presentation onto index cards. It may help students feel comfortable including only word clues on their overheads if they can write out the whole sentence that goes with it. Some students may not need to write down their parts, but others may find it a very important confidence-building tool.

9. Groups who finish early can begin practicing their presentations.

Discussion Questions

1. What are the differences between a great presentation, an adequate presentation, and a weak presentation?

2. How do visual aids improve a presentation? How can visual aids detract from a presentation?

3. What kinds of visual aids are fun? What kind of visual aids help you understand the material? Think about the visual aids your teacher uses.

4. How is written language different from oral language?

5. What techniques help keep an audience's attention? *Humor, intonation, loud voices, pictures, enthusiasm.*

6. What kinds of questions might someone ask about your project?

7. Which scientific words will the audience be familiar with? With which will they be unfamiliar?

Preparing Your Presentation Worksheet

Put a check in the box when you have completed the task.

 1. Organize your presentation: What do you want to say? In what order do you want to say it? Who will say what?

☐ **2.** Make a list of each overhead you will need to make.

3. Create overheads for each section of your presentation. Write out the script, or what you will actually say, for each section.

Use word clues or bulleted lists on overheads. No long sentences or paragraphs. Use HUGE font!

 Title

☐ **Outline of Presentation**—How is the presentation organized? Instead of just saying Introduction, Methods, Results, Discussion, try to think of creative titles for the different parts of your presentation—for example, "What You Need to Know about Ants." Questions can be fun—for example, "What Did We Study?".

 Introduction—Some facts; background about your subject or why you are studying this subject; research question; hypotheses.

 Methods—Exactly what you did. Use a diagram, a map, a picture, a description of the study site.

☐ **Results**—Tables of data, graphs of data, statistics.

☐ **Discussion/Conclusions**—What do you think your results mean? Why did you find these results? What would you like to study next?

 ☐ **4. PRACTICE!**

Practicing Your Presentation Worksheet

Number the overheads in the order you will be presenting them.

Number the index cards (on which you have written what you will be saying) with the same numbers.

Find a partner, go to a quiet corner, and practice giving the presentation to each other. Remember your order. Try to tell about your project without reading every word from your cards. If you get stuck, you can look at the card for ideas.

Presentation Tips:

- Look at the audience, *not* at your overheads.
- Speak slowly.
- Explain complicated words.
- Keep hands out of pockets.
- Stand to the side of the overhead projector so you don't block the audience's view.
- Stop and smile if you are nervous—you don't need to fill all the time with words.
- Give the audience time to read each overhead. It's OK to stand quietly while they look at a map or graph.
- Describe the axes on each graph *before* you talk about the information.
- Practice and time your presentation (here and at home).

Have FUN up there and the audience will have FUN with you!

LTRP: Practicing Research Presentations

Day 40

Overview

The students have an opportunity to practice their presentations in front of the class or another class. The goal is to polish the presentations and to reduce any feelings of stage fright. Treat this as a dress rehearsal if you can. Groups will go in the same order they will follow for the formal presentations. Printing a program that gives the order of presentations helps students keep track of when to give their presentations. At the end of the practice session, the class will discuss ideas to improve the presentations.

Focus Question

How can we improve our presentations?

Science Skills

■ Students should be able to give constructive comments on other groups' presentations.

■ Students should be able to listen to comments about their presentation from classmates.

Background

For background information describing the concepts in this lesson, see "Planning for the Final Celebration," page xvi, and "Oral Presentations," page 176.

Materials

■ overhead projector

■ screen

■ pointer (optional)

Development of Lesson

1. Give the students 10 minutes to get their overheads and index cards in order. They may also have time to rehearse their part quickly.

2. Set up the classroom so there is a stage area and an audience area. Hand out copies of the program or post the order of presentations on the board.

3. Ask the class if they can think of any terms used in the presentations that the audience might not understand (e.g., hypothesis/null hypothesis, replication, t-test, p-value). Ask the class how they can explain these terms to the audience. One suggestion is to prepare overheads with definitions of scientific words. The first group can use these to introduce the audience to potentially unfamiliar terms. Example of such overheads are found in Appendix A. Use the example overheads or prepare new overheads as a class. Have volunteers or the first group practice explaining the terms to the audience.

4. Give a brief introduction to the audience about the project, as you will do at the formal presentations. This is a chance for the teacher to practice and for the students to hear the teacher's impression of the project and student achievement.

5. Let the presentations begin. You may want to take notes to remind certain groups or individuals about specific points. Things to watch for include:

- volume, speaking to the back of the room
- smooth transitions between speakers
- legible overheads
- standing still while speaking
- looking at audience, not at overhead
- allowing audience time to look at or read each overhead
- standing quietly when not speaking
- clear and thorough descriptions of project

6. At the end of each presentation, allow time for several questions.

7. At the end of all the presentations, discuss the positive aspects of the presentations. What did the students see that they liked? What made it easier to do the presentation?

8. Ask the students if they feel ready for the formal presentations. If not, you may want to arrange some time for them to practice again.

   Note: Practicing the presentations in front of a different class is a great way of keeping the students serious and focused on their presentations. If the other class will be doing the curriculum in the next semester or school year, watching the presentations is a great introduction to the projects.

Discussion Questions

1. What techniques have you used to help keep the audience interested?

2. What techniques do you use to feel less nervous?

3. What makes a good presentation?

4. How do you feel as a speaker standing in front of the audience?

5. What kinds of questions could someone ask you about your project?

6. Make a list of general tips for someone to remember when speaking in front of a group.

7. In what types of jobs might you be asked to speak in front of a group?

LTRP:
CELEBRATION NIGHT

Overview

The final presentation is a highlight of *The Truth about Science* curriculum. Including the final presentation motivates many students to do the best work they can. It is also a way to showcase and celebrate the students' hard work throughout the curriculum. Include the students in the planning of this evening as much as possible. They can create invitations to take home to parents and give to others at the school. Posters are displayed by taping them to the walls of the room or hallway. The students can set up tables with examples of some of the activities they did during the curriculum, such as the Ooze, paper towel, and worm experiments. You may want to have a guest register book for visitors to sign in and write comments. Food and beverages increase the celebratory atmosphere.

Focus Question

N/A

Science Skills

■ Students should be able to stand in front of an audience and give a formal research presentation.

Background

For background information describing the concepts in this lesson, see "Planning for the Final Celebration," page xvi; "Poster Presentations," page 176; and "Oral Presentations," page 176.

Materials

■ place for presentations

■ overhead projector

■ screen

■ microphone

■ extension cord

■ pointer (optional)

■ food and beverages (optional)

■ printed program

■ award certificates (provided)

National Science Teachers Association

Development of Lesson

1. Before the celebration begins:

   - tape posters to wall in presentation room or in hallway

   - set up tables with some of the activities done during the curriculum (e.g., Ooze, paper towel, worm experiments)

   - photocopy and fill out award certificates

   - set up overhead, screen, and microphone and make sure everything works without blowing a fuse

   - set out programs listing the order of the presentations

2. Allow 30 minutes for students and parents to arrive and view posters and demonstrations. Then begin the oral presentations. (For example, invite people to come at 6:30 p.m. and begin the presentations at 7:00 p.m.) Do your best to keep to the times you have scheduled.

3. When the audience is seated and the students are ready to begin the presentations, welcome the parents. Introduce the overall project and praise the students for their hard work and achievement.

4. Have several students define words that will be used in all presentations (e.g., replication, control and treatment, null hypothesis, p-value) before beginning the presentations. Alternatively, you can give this responsibility to the first group.

5. Presentations generally take three to five minutes per group.

6. Solicit one or two questions from the audience per group, depending on the length of a presentation.

7. Give out award certificates at the end of each presentation.

Outstanding Achievement in Science

awarded to

Promising Young Scientist

for enthusiastically demonstrating skills and competency
in completing a science research project

SCHOOL

DATE

PRINCIPAL

TEACHER

APPENDIX A:
Definitions of Statistical Terms

The definitions in this appendix can be photocopied onto transparencies and used by the teacher for defining or reviewing terminology in class.

The definitions can also be used by students at the beginning of the celebration night. The teacher may ask several students to define these terms for the audience at the beginning of the program. Students may choose to use photocopies of these pages or of portions of these pages. Students can also use these pages as a guide for creating their own definitions.

RESEARCH QUESTION

- A research question compares two things.

- A research question must be answered using quantitative data.

HYPOTHESIS

■ A hypothesis is a prediction about what you expect your research results to show.

■ To simplify the statistical testing, our hypotheses predict that there will be a difference between the two things that we are comparing.

NULL HYPOTHESIS

- The null hypothesis is the opposite of the hypothesis.

- Our null hypotheses state that there will be no difference between the two things that we are comparing.

- We will use our data to choose between our hypothesis and our null hypothesis.

- We start out assuming that the null hypothesis is true. If we get data that would be very unlikely under the null hypothesis, then we can conclude that there is a difference between the things that we are comparing.

National Science Teachers Association

P-VALUE

■ We used statistical tests to decide if we thought our hypothesis or our null hypothesis was true. The result of the statistical test was a p-value.

■ A p-value is calculated from three things: the averages of the data for the two things we're comparing, the variability of the data, and the number of samples we collected.

■ A p-value describes the chances of getting our data if the null hypothesis is true.

APPENDIX B:
Example Posters

These example posters can be used to help students imagine what a poster presentation might look like. The examples can be photocopied onto transparencies, passed around, or pinned up to a wall. The first poster was created with combined data from two classes for the Wigglin' Worm lesson (Days 13, 14). These data are used again in Appendix C: Worm Presentation. The second page of example posters are student posters. The selection was chosen to provide as broad a range of creative ideas as possible.

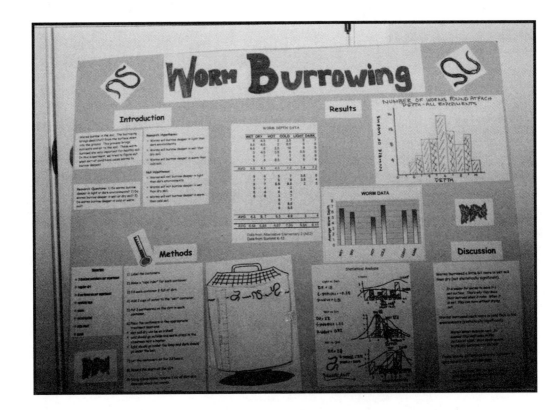

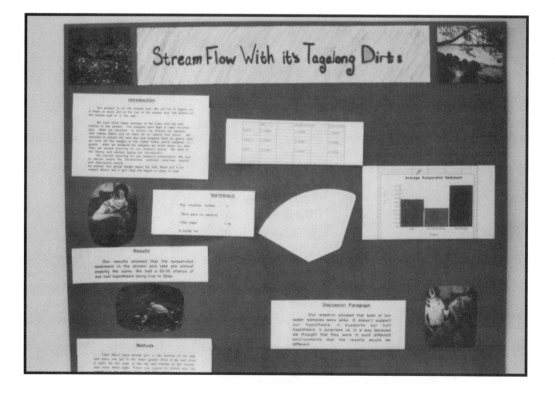

APPENDIX C:
Worm Presentation

The pages in this appendix are intended to be photocopied onto transparencies and used to create a sample scientific presentation for the data from Wigglin' Worms (Days 13, 14). The data in this presentation were collected by two classes that completed the experiment. The main points of the presentation are outlined in the overheads, but the teacher can modify the presentation as needed. When actually giving the presentation to the class, the teacher can add verbal details not included in the overheads. Students should also be encouraged to use the visual aids as an audience guide rather than as a script.

National Science Teachers Association

Worm Burrowing Behavior Experiments

By

Ima Student

Presentation Outline

Introduction: Who cares about earthworms?

Methods: What did we do?

Results: What happened when we did our experiments?

Discussion: What do the results tell us about earthworm behavior?

Earthworms
Lumbricus terrestris

Population: 50,000 earthworms per acre of moist soil.

Habitat: Moist, loose soils where they can dig deep, dark, long, narrow burrows.

Biology: 100 or more body segments, setae (leg-like bristles), no lungs, sightless, earless.

Predators: Birds and burrowing animals.

Adaptations: Can re-grow body rings; breathe through their skin; mucus on body (for sliding); setae (for holding on inside burrows); feel vibrations (alerts them to predators).

Benefits of Earthworms

■ Bring organic debris from surface into burrows.

■ Mix soil.

■ Aerate soil.

■ Burrows bring in nutrient-rich rainwater.

■ Castings provide 18 tons of nutrient-rich soil per *acre* per *year*.

■ Dead worm bodies provide extra nutrients (minerals) to the soil.

National Science Teachers Association

Research Questions:

1. Do worms burrow deeper in light or dark environments?

2. Do worms burrow deeper in wet or dry soil?

3. Do worms burrow deeper in cold or hot soil?

Hypotheses:

- Worms will burrow to different depths in light versus dark environments.

- Worms will burrow to different depths in wet versus dry soil.

- Worms will burrow to different depths in hot versus cold soil.

Null Hypotheses:

- Worms will burrow to the same depth in light and dark environments.

- Worms will burrow to the same depth in wet and dry soil.

- Worms will burrow to the same depth in hot and cold soil.

Materials

- 2 identical containers per experiment (large yogurt containers or 2 L soda bottles with tops cut off work well)

- regular dirt (enough to fill all the containers at least ¾ full)

- 6 earthworms per experiment

- masking tape

- spoons

- extra bucket

- pencil

- measuring cups

- water

- metric rulers

Methods

1. Labeled the containers (wet/dry; hot/cold; or dark/light).

2. Made centimeter tape rulers with masking tape and placed on outside of containers.

3. Filled each container ¾ full with dirt.

4. Added 2 tsp. to each container. (Added 2 more tsp. of water to the "wet" container, if doing the wet/dry experiment.)

5. Put three earthworms on top of dirt in each container.

6. Set containers in treatment locations.

7. Waited 23 hours.

8. Recorded the depth of the dirt.

9. Removed dirt 1 cm at a time, checking for worms.

10. Recorded depth of each worm located.

Results
Data Table

	WET	DRY	HOT	COLD	LIGHT	DARK
	8	4.5	2	3.5	9	7
	8.5	4.5	2	8.5	9	8
	9.5	8	2.5	10	9	9
	3	4.5	3.5	6	5.5	5
	6	7	7	7	6	6
	6	8	8.5	8	6	8
	5	6	5	7	3.5	5
	7	7	6	8	3.5	4
	9	7	6.5	8.5	2	3
	5	4	4	3		
	6	4	6	4		
	6	6	3	7		
			5	7		
			6	8.5		
			6	9.5		
AVG	6.58	5.88	4.87	7.03	5.94	6.11

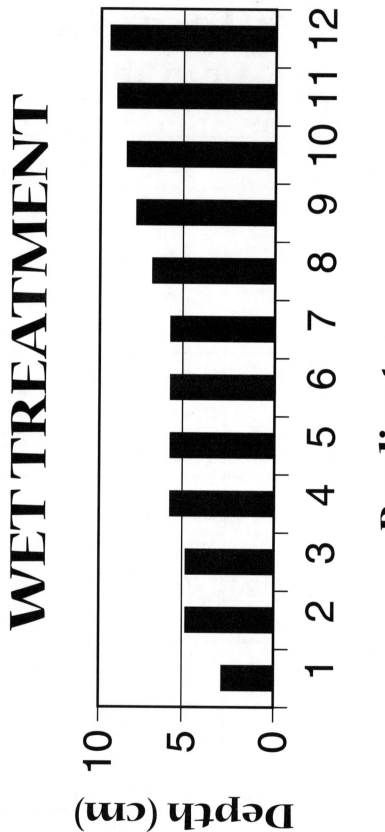

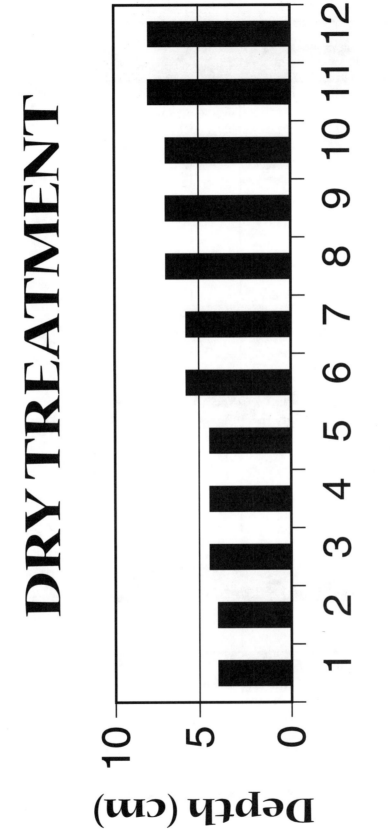

DRY TREATMENT

Depth (cm)

Replicates

WORM DATA

Average Worm Depth

WET DRY · HOT COLD · LIGHT DARK

Statistical Testing

Light versus Dark   P-Value = 0.81

There is an 81% chance of seeing data like these if the null hypothesis is true.

Wet versus Dry   P-Value = 0.32

There is a 32% chance of seeing data like these if the null hypothesis is true.

Hot versus Cold   P-Value = 0.007

There is only a 0.7% chance of seeing data like these if the null hypothesis is true. It is so unlikely that we can reject our null hypothesis!

Discussion

There was no difference in worm behavior in light versus dark environments.

Worms don't have eyes. Even if they can sense light, once under the soil, the worms probably cannot tell the difference between light and dark.

Worms burrowed a little bit more in wet soil than dry (not statistically significant).

It is easier for worms to move in a wet surface. That's why they leave their burrows when it rains. They can move without drying out. Dry soil in the experiment may not have been dry enough to alter movement of worms.

Worms burrowed much more in cold than in hot environments (statistically significant).

Worms cannot tolerate heat. In summer they only come to the surface at night. Most deaths occur in the dry, warm time of the year.

APPENDIX D:
How to Make Tables and Graphs Using Microsoft Works

I nstructions for using Microsoft Works are included in this appendix for teachers who choose to have their students produce computer-generated graphs. Familiarity with whatever graphing software the students use is essential. This appendix is a good way for teachers to familiarize themselves with MS Works before the lesson and can be used for student reference during class. Students should be able to answer many of their own questions by referring to the information on this sheet. A copy can be kept with each group's LTRP materials for easy reference. At the end of the appendix is a list of tips for saving documents on the computer. It may be valuable to go over these tips as a group before students begin working on the computers.

TABLES

Open Microsoft Works under the rainbow Apple icon in the upper left-hand corner of the screen or on the icon on the desktop.

◼ Double-click on the Spreadsheet icon. You should see a page that looks something like this, but with more rows and columns:

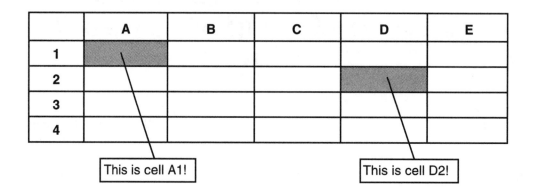

This is cell A1!

This is cell D2!

◼ Each box in the spreadsheet is called a cell and has its own address. For example, the first cell in the upper left-hand corner of the page is cell A1. The next cell to the right is B1. The first cell below cell B1 is cell B2.

◼ To enter your data, type the title of each column in B1 and C1. Skip cell A1 and type the replicates (locations, observations, days, etc.) in A2, A3,... for as many replicates as you have. Follow the example below.

	A	B	C
1		Coniferous Trees	Deciduous Trees
2	Location 1	12	55
3	Location 2	7	27
4	Location 3	10	34

Example Table

◼ The labels (Coniferous Trees, Deciduous Trees, and Locations 1–3) will be used by the computer to make the graph. Labels can contain letters and/or numbers. The data (in cells B2–B4 and C2–C4) can only be written in numbers. You will use your table to make the graph.

◼ The spreadsheet program can also calculate averages. To calculate the average of each of the columns in the table given above, type =average(B2:B4) in cell B5. Then hit return. You can copy and paste this formula into cell C5 and the spreadsheet will automatically redo the calculations for the data in column C. When you hit return, the average is displayed rather than the formula. To see the formula, click on the cell.

	A	B	C
1		Coniferous Trees	Deciduous Trees
2	Location 1	12	55
3	Location 2	7	27
4	Location 3	10	34
5	AVERAGE	=average(B2:B4)	=average(C2:C4)

This is what you type.

	A	B	C
1		Coniferous Trees	Deciduous Trees
2	Location 1	12	55
3	Location 2	7	27
4	Location 3	10	34
5	AVERAGE	9.666667	38.666667

This is the average the computer calculates after you hit "RETURN."

GRAPHS

■ You will use your table to make the graph. First, highlight all the cells with labels and data. (Highlighting the cells means to drag the mouse across the cells while holding the clicker down.) Your table should look like this after you have highlighted everything:

Highlighting darkens the cells in a table.

	A	B	C
1		Coniferous Trees	Deciduous Trees
2	Location 1	12	55
3	Location 2	7	27
4	Location 3	10	34
5	AVERAGE	9.67	38.67

■ Go to New Chart under the Chart menu. When you let go of the clicker on New Chart, the computer will display a graph of your data. The graph will look like this:

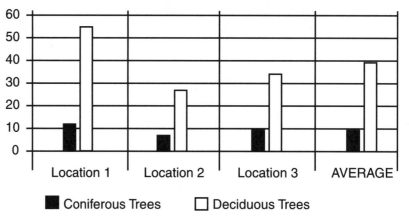

■ To make formatting changes in the graph, go to Define Chart under the Chart menu. In this dialogue box you can write a specific title for your graph. You can choose the type of graph (pie, line, column). You can change the scale of the y-axis (vertical axis) by entering a minimum and maximum value in the boxes at the bottom of the dialogue box. You can change whether the rows or columns are on the y-axis by choosing Data by Rows or Data by Columns.

■ Once you have a graph displayed, you must tell the computer when you want to switch from working on the graph to the table (and vice versa). To switch from the graph to the table, click on the cross button (:) in the upper left-hand corner of the graph toolbox. To switch from the table to the graph, click on the pencil button (0) in the upper right-hand corner of the graph toolbox. You must always save and print from the table/spreadsheet function.

Graphing Research Data

1. Make three graphs of your data:

    In the first graph, include only the data for your first treatment type (column B, Coniferous Trees, in the example above.) To do this, select New Chart under the Chart menu, then go back to Define Chart. Type in a different title. Select the Data by Columns button, and below it enter column B and rows 2 through 4. In the box that says Legend, enter row 1 and in the Labels box enter column A. Click okay and check out the graph.

    In the second graph, include only the data for your second treatment type (column C, Deciduous Trees, in the example above.) Follow the directions for the first graph, but enter column C and rows 2 through 4. Be sure the scale is the same as the first two graphs.

    The last graph will show only your averages. Follow the directions for the second graph, only this time enter column B and column C, row 5. Change the maximum value of the y-axis to the same number you used for the first graph. You can change the scale for the y-axis at the bottom of the dialogue box under Define Chart.

2. Now you can change the labels on the x- and y-axes of all three graphs. Click on the A in the graph toolbox. Then click on the word "Value" or the word "Category" on the graph. Delete the letters and type in new labels. After entering the new title, click on the arrow in the graph toolbox. If you want to move the new label around, click on the new label and drag it. If you want to change the shape of the new label, click on one of the black squares and drag to make a different shape.

    Don't be afraid to play around and try different things. You will learn more about your data and more about the spreadsheet capabilities.

Tips On Saving Documents

■   To save to a disk, put a floppy disk in the disk drive. Select Save As under the File menu. Click on the Desktop button on the right side of the dialogue box. Double-click on the name of the disk on the left side of the box. Then type the name of the document in the box under Save Current Document As: and click once on the Save button.

■   To save to the hard drive, select Save As under the File menu. Click and hold on the up and down arrows to the right of the hard drive file listed in the box in the upper left-hand side of the dialogue box. Select a file on the hard drive to save your document in and release the mouse. Then type the name of the document in the box under Save Current Document As: and click once on the Save button.

    Be sure to give your document a name that describes what it is. Do not use a name that you have used previously. (If you try to save a document with the same name as a previously saved document, the new document will write over the old one. The old document will be lost forever!)

APPENDIX E:
Scenario-Based Assessment Questions

The following scenarios can be used independently or combined to make a more specific assessment tool. For example, a teacher might use five questions from one scenario as a summative assessment. Another teacher might use questions about experimental design from four different scenarios as a formative assessment. Multiple-choice, short answer, and essay questions are provided for each scenario. Questions range from simple to difficult.

The scenarios are loosely organized to emphasize material from each of the first three sections of the curriculum. No assessment scenarios are provided for the final section of the curriculum, Presentation of Research Projects, because it is, in and of itself, a summative assessment.

Scenario for Section I: Research Questions and Hypotheses

Snail Research Project: A group of students was studying snails. They wanted to know about snail movements.

1. List three things you could measure quantitatively about snail movements.

    Possible answers: *Travel speed, time spent moving versus sitting still, number of times the snail crossed a line, time to leave a circle of a given radius, amount of slime left behind.*

2. Which of the following are qualitative descriptions of snail movement (circle all that apply):

    (a) wiggliness (b) attractiveness (c) stickiness (d) boringness

    Answer: *All of the above.*

3. Choose one of the qualitative measures you circled above and describe a possible technique for making it quantitative.

    Possible answers: *Wiggliness could be measured as the number of times a snail crosses a line. Attractiveness could be measured on a scale from 1 to 10. Stickiness could be measured as the weight of things that can be held to the bottom of a bottle with one teaspoon of snail slime. Boringness could be measured as the number of people who fall asleep while watching it move.*

4. What two characteristics determine whether a question is a testable research question?

    Answer: *It has a comparison and a quantitative measurement.*

5. State a research question about snail movements.

    Possible answers: *Are snails faster on wet versus dry surfaces? Going uphill versus downhill? Do snail movements create more slime on a smooth or a rough surface?*

6. State the null hypothesis for your research question.

    Possible answers: *There is no difference between the speed of snails on wet versus dry surfaces. There is no difference in the speed of snails going uphill versus downhill. There is no difference in the amount of slime created by snails on smooth versus rough surfaces.*

7. What types of information would go into an introduction paragraph for this research project?

    Possible answers: *Snail life history information, reasons why snail behavior might differ by surface type, reasons why this group wanted to study snails, anatomy of a snail.*

Scenario for Section II: Experimental Design

Balloon Research Project: A group of students was interested in the effect of color on the time balloons stayed inflated. They thought that balloons of some colors would hold air longer than balloons of other colors. They planned to measure the time it takes for 10 white balloons and 10 black balloons to deflate.

1. Write an example methods paragraph for this experiment.

    Possible answer: *Make a 10-cm and a 5-cm hole in a piece of cardboard. Blow up 10 white and 10 black balloons until they are 10 cm in diameter. Add air until the balloons just fit inside the 10-cm hole. Every morning test whether the balloons fit into the 5-cm hole. Record the number of days. Materials: a piece of cardboard, a pair of scissors, a ruler, and 20 balloons.*

2. List three things that you would need to control for to do this experiment carefully.

    Possible answers: *Air temperature, same brand of balloon, same size of balloon, same person blowing up all the balloons, keeping balloons in the same place, using the same measuring device for all balloons.*

3. Which of the following describes the two treatments in this experiment:

    (a) two sizes of hole (b) two people blowing up the balloons (c) two colors of balloon (d) number of days until balloon is deflated

    Answer: *(c) two colors of balloon.*

4. Jessie decides to save money and brings in five black balloons left over from his birthday party. Is it a good idea to use these in the experiment? Why or why not?

    Answer: *No, the balloons from the birthday party might be a different size, shape, or material from the ones the students are studying and that would make it difficult to detect the effect of color.*

5. Why not simplify the experiment and just use one balloon of each color?

    Possible Answers: *We would expect that all black balloons, for example, would take slightly different numbers of days to deflate. In order to measure the full range, we need more samples. It will help us to answer the research question if we observe more samples. More samples will make it easier to decide if the null hypothesis is true.*

Scenario for Section III: Analyzing and Summarizing Results

Tree Diameter Project: A group of students wanted to find out if the trees in the playground were exceptionally big. Their research question was "Do trees in the playground have bigger diameters than trees in our backyards?" They measured five trees in the playground and then they each measured one tree in their own backyards.

1. They will need to choose random trees in the playground and in their backyards. Why?

   Answer: *It would be very easy for them to bias their results by choosing the biggest trees in the playground and the smallest trees in their backyards.*

2. Describe a method for choosing a random tree.

   Possible Answers: *They could list all the trees in the playground on slips of paper and pull five out of a hat. Blindfolded, they could throw a dart at a map of the playground. They could spin in a circle with their eyes closed and when their friend (also with eyes closed) says, "Stop," they could walk in that direction to the first tree.*

3. Here is the data they collected. Calculate the average diameter for each treatment:

   Playground: 32 cm, 50 cm, 33 cm, 21 cm, 54 cm

   Backyard: 20 cm, 18 cm, 68 cm, 15 cm, 31 cm

   Answer: *Playground = 38 cm, Backyard = 30.4*

4. Graph the observations for the two treatments on the axes below:

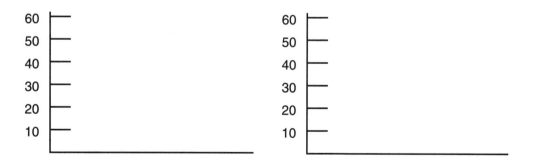

   Teacher Ideas: *Students should be able to graph each of the five observations on the two axes. You can choose to suggest that they label the axes or test whether they remember. You can also decide whether or not you want to provide ready-made axes or have the students figure out how to divide up the axes. You may also want to ask them to graph the two averages.*

5. List three things you can learn about the research results from observing these graphs.

   Possible answers: *The trees on the playground are generally larger. One backyard tree was much larger than all the other trees. There is a lot of variability in tree size for both playground and backyard trees. All the trees were smaller than 60 cm in diameter.*

6. State the null hypothesis. What do you conclude about the null hypothesis? Is it likely to be true? Explain your answer.

   Possible answers: *There is no difference in tree size between trees in the playground and trees in backyards. Students may conclude that the null hypothesis is true based on the means. A more sophisticated answer might note that aside from the one large tree, all backyard trees were very small. Other students might note that not very many samples were taken or that there is a lot of variability in the data so it is difficult to decide.*

7. What three pieces of information from the data help you decide if the null hypothesis is true?

   Answer: *The difference between the averages, the number of observations, and the variability of the data.*

8. Define a p-value and estimate it for these data. Explain your answer.

   Answer: *A p-value describes the odds of getting these data if the null hypothesis is true. Estimates should be in the range from 0.2 to 0.8. Similar logic should be provided for this question as for question 6.*